Joseph Barnabas
His Life and Legacy

Bernd Kollmann

Translated by
Miranda Henry

A Michael Glazier Book

LITURGICAL PRESS
Collegeville, Minnesota

www.litpress.org

A Michael Glazier Book published by Liturgical Press

Cover design by David Manahan, O.S.B. Icon of Saint Barnabas courtesy of Holy Transfiguration Monastery, Brookline, Massachusetts.

This book was originally published in German by Verlag Katholisches Bibelwerk GmbH, Stuttgart, under the title *Joseph Barnabas: Leben und Wirkungsgeschichte.* © 1998 by Verlag Katholisches Bibelwerk. All rights reserved.

1   2   3   4   5   6   7   8

Library of Congress Cataloging-in-Publication Data

Kollmann, Bernd.
    [Joseph Barnabas. English]
    Joseph Barnabas: his life and legacy / Bernd Kollmann ; translated by Miranda Henry.
      p. cm.
    "A Michael Glazier book."
    Includes bibliographical references (p.   ).
    ISBN 0-8146-5170-4
    1. Barnabas, Apostle, Saint. 2. Christian saints—Cyprus—Biography.
  I. Title.

BS2452.B28K64 2004
226.6'092—dc22   2004004196

Contents

But all honored him because of the divine grace surrounding his countenance. For his face was like that of an angel and his character ascetic. His eyebrows had grown together, and he had sparkling eyes, which did not look around grimly but rather remained piously downcast. His mouth was venerable, and from his lips came sweet sounds, trickling down like honey—and they never emitted a superfluous sound. His gait was measured and free of arrogant swaggering, and he was through and through a pure pillar of Christ, this apostle Barnabas, in whom all the virtues shone.

Alexander Monachus, *Laudatio Barnabae* 25:469–78

Foreword

While Peter, Paul, and increasingly also James have dominated New Testament scholarship, Joseph Barnabas has received relatively little attention. This is all the more astonishing given that he, more than anyone else, played a substantial role in every stage of early Christianity and had a decisive influence on the fate of the Church in the first century C.E. The following study attempts to free Joseph Barnabas from his undeserved obscurity and place him in the proper light as a founding figure of the Christian Church, as well as a sponsor of the apostle Paul. Of particular note in this study is the examination of the early Church's Barnabas tradition.

The idea for this study arose out of an introductory course entitled "Paul, the Apostle to the Gentiles," which I taught in the winter semester of 1996–97 at RWTH Aachen and in the summer semester of 1997 at the Georg-August-Universität at Göttingen. It became clear to me that Barnabas' influence on the development of the pre-Pauline tradition, as well as on Paul himself, had not been sufficiently appreciated by scholars. Dr. W. Reinbold of Göttingen commented critically on the entire manuscript and in several cases helped make my position more precise. I thank Prof. Dr. W. Deuse of Cologne/Siegen for the numerous suggestions for improving my translations of the *Acts of Barnabas* and the *Laudatio Barnabae* of Alexander Monachus.

Wolfsburg/Siegen, Easter 1998   Bernd Kollmann

Introduction

When, after a protracted struggle, the legitimacy of the mission to the Gentiles (without imposing the requirement of male circumcision) finally won the day at the so-called Council of Jerusalem and consequently became a decisive influence in the future of the Church, five people (according to Paul's account in Galatians) took part in reaching the epochal agreement (Gal 2:9). On one side stood James, Peter/Cephas, and John as the three "pillars" of the Jerusalem congregation, and on the other stood Paul and Joseph Barnabas, representing the congregation of Antioch.

On the basis of their significance in early Christian texts and in still greater measure on account of their substantial historical influence, Peter and Paul are indisputably *the* outstanding figures of early Christianity. Ferdinand Christian Baur once interpreted the entire history of early Christianity in terms of the contrast between Peter and Paul, with the "ideal of the Catholic Church" serving as the point of reconciliation.[1] As the underlying image of Peter as representative of a strict, legalistic Jewish Christianity became untenable, James, the Lord's brother, began to attract increasing attention as the true leading authority of the early Christian community.[2] It became clear that early Christianity's most significant line of division, based on contrasting positions toward the Torah, ran between *James* and Paul, with Peter acting as a mediating figure between these two extremes.[3]

---

[1] Ferdinand Christian Baur, *The Church History of the First Three Centuries*, trans. Allan Menzies (London: Williams and Norgate, 1878).

[2] Cf. Martin Hengel, "Jakobus der Herrenbruder," in Erich Gräßer and Otto Merk, eds., *Glaube und Eschatologie. Festschrift Werner Georg Kümmel zum 80. Geburtstag* (Tübingen: J.C.B. Mohr [Paul Siebeck], 1985) 71–104; Wilhelm Pratscher, *Der Herrenbruder Jakobus und die Jakobustradition* (Göttingen: Vandenhoeck & Ruprecht, 1987), *passim*.

[3] Cf. Lothar Wehr, *Petrus und Paulus—Kontrahenten und Partner: Die beiden Apostel im Spiegel des Neuen Testaments, der Apostolischen Väter und frühere Zeugnisse ihrer Verehrung* (Münster: Aschendorff, 1996) 376–87.

1

The two remaining participants in the Council of Jerusalem, John, son of Zebedee, and Joseph Barnabas, have received differing amounts of attention, though in both cases less than the aforementioned three outstanding figures of early Christianity. In the case of John this is readily understood, as beyond his being a disciple, his participation in the Council of Jerusalem as one of the three leading figures of the Christian community, and his presumed martyrdom (Mark 10:38-40), essentially nothing is reliably known about him.[4] Far less understandable, however, is the remarkable lack of interest scholars have shown in Barnabas. His significant role in the Acts of the Apostles and his frequent mention in the Pauline epistles shed light not only on aspects of his biography but also on his theological profile, placing beyond doubt his importance for the history of early Christianity.

That Barnabas belongs among the truly significant individuals in early Christianity has occasionally been recognized.[5] The most recent comprehensive scholarly study dedicated to him dates from 1876[6] and can scarcely be considered adequate today, not only on account of its considerable age but also because of its largely uncritical approach toward ecclesiastical tradition. In light of this background, our attempt to examine the development of Joseph Barnabas, theologically as well as biographically, requires no special justification. Of particular note in relation to this is the early Christian historiography of Joseph Barnabas, which already indirectly reflects his outstanding importance in the earliest years of Christianity. A glance at the sources collected below—which make no claim to completeness—ought at least to qualify the

---

[4] Cf. L. Oberlinner, "Johannes (Apostel)," *Neues Bibel-Lexicon* II (1995) 350–53.

[5] Hans Conzelmann, *History of Primitive Christianity,* trans. John E. Steely (Nashville: Abingdon, 1973) 158: "The couple of fragmentary notes about him do not correspond to his actual significance. In truth he was one of the most important personalities of the primitive church." Alfons Weiser, *Die Apostelgeschichte* (Gütersloh: Gerd Mohn, 1981) 1:138: "Barnabas is one of the leading men of early Christian missionary history."

[6] Otto Braunsberger, *Der Apostel Barnabas: Sein Leben und der ihm beigelegte Brief* (Mainz: Florian Kupferberg, 1876). The most useful recent works with regard to Barnabas are Conzelmann, *History of Primitive Christianity* (see n. 5 above); Wolf-Henning Ollrog, *Paulus und seine Mitarbeiter: Untersuchungen zur Theorie und Praxis der paulinischen Mission* (Neukirchen-Vluyn: Neukirchener Verlag, 1979) 14–17, 206–15; Walter Radl, "Das 'Apostelkonzil' und seine Nachgeschichte, dargestellt am Weg des Barnabas," *ThQ* 162 (1982) 45–61 (45 n. 1 surveys earlier literature); Martin Hengel and Anna Maria Schwemer, *Paul between Damascus and Antioch: The Unknown Years* (London: S.C.M., 1997) 205–24. Cf. also Ernst Haenchen, "Barnabas," *RGG* I (1957) 879; Walter Radl, "Βαρναβᾶς," *EDNT* 1:199; Walter Radl, "Barnabas," *Neues Bibel-Lexicon* I (1991) 244ff.; J.B. Daniels, "Barnabas," *ABD* (1992) 1:610–11; Christoph Markschies, "Barnabas," *Der Neue Pauly. Enzyklopädie der Antike* (1997) 2:452. The *Theologische Realenzyklopädie* does not include an article on Barnabas.

asserTning_

assertion of Richard A. Lipsius that the older tradition of the Church remained "nearly silent" with regard to Barnabas.[7]

The Pre-Christian Barnabas

Birth and Sources

Joseph, also called Barnabas in the early community (Acts 4:36), emerges suddenly into the history of early Christianity on the occasion of his sale of a field. The course of his life prior to this watershed event remains largely obscure. However, at least the approximate date of his birth can be determined. Since Joseph Barnabas was probably older than Paul, who was born around the start of the Common Era,[8] he was likely born toward the end of the first century B.C.E. Knowledge of the intellectual and theological formation of the pre-Christian Barnabas would be of inestimable value for our understanding of the Christian Barnabas, but from the outset the amount of information preserved regarding the approximately forty years of Joseph Barnabas' life preceding his entry into the Christian community has been strictly limited. The main source remains Acts 4:36, with gaps in his biography filled in by the legends of Alexander Monachus (*Laudatio* 9:145–15:270). All the same, even the meager biographical data of Acts 4:36, "Joseph . . . a Levite, a native of Cyprus," offer clues to the political, economic, religious, and cultural framework that influenced Joseph Barnabas' development.

Origins in Cyprus

According to Acts 4:36 Joseph Barnabas was "a native (τῷ γένει) of Cyprus," that is, he was probably born there.[9] It cannot be determined whether the city of his birth was Salamis.[10]

[7] Richard Adelbert Lipsius, *Die apokryphen Apostelgeschichten und Apostellegenden: Ein Beitrag zur altchristlichen Literaturgeschichte* (Braunschweig: C. A. Schwetschke und Sohn, 1884) II.2.270.

[8] The determination of Paul's date of birth near the start of the Common Era is based on the letter to Philemon, written in the 50s, where Paul characterizes himself as "now an old man" (Phlm 9). Cf. Joachim Gnilka, *Paulus von Tarsus: Apostel und Zeuge* (Freiburg: Herder, 1996) 23.

[9] Τῷ γένει not only implies the origin of his family there but also permits the conclusion that he was born in Cyprus (Hans Conzelmann, *Acts of the Apostles: A Commentary on the Acts of the Apostles,* trans. James Limburg, A. Thomas Kraabel, and Donald H. Juel; ed. Eldon Jay Epp, with Christopher R. Matthews. Hermeneia [Philadelphia: Fortress, 1987] 36), which the early church accepted as self-evident. According to Epiphanius, *Panarion Haer.* XXX.25:6-9 (similar to Alexander Monachus, *Laudatio* 9:149-51), Barnabas' family left Palestine for Cyprus during the reign of Antiochus Epiphanes (175–164 B.C.E.) or at a later date, because of war.

[10] According to Terence Bruce Mitford, "Roman Cyprus," in *ANRW* I.7,2 (1980) 1380 ("Barnabas [was] a native of Salamis"). No source material exists to support this. In

Cyprus, the third-largest island in the Mediterranean Sea, had been ruled by the Ptolemies since the end of the fourth century B.C.E. and had become increasingly Hellenized. In 58 B.C.E. the Roman Senate, led by Cato, annexed Cyprus, and it was subsequently administered as an appendix of the province of Cilicia by the provincial governors. The most prominent of these governors was Cicero, who held office in 51–50 B.C.E. Around 48–47 B.C.E. Julius Caesar returned the island to the Ptolemies, and it was ruled *de facto* by Cleopatra VII, whose right to occupy Cyprus was recognized by Antony in 36 B.C.E. (Plutarch, *Vit. Ant.* 36:3; Dio Chrysostom, *Hist.* XLIX 32:5). This Ptolemaic restoration remained, however, only a historical intermezzo. Following the battle of Actium and the deaths of Antony and Cleopatra, Octavian placed Cyprus under his direct control in 30 B.C.E. before establishing the island in 22 B.C.E. as a senatorial province governed by a proconsul chosen annually.

During the period of Ptolemaic rule in Cyprus a large number of Jews immigrated to the island, beginning at the latest in the reign of Philadelphos (283–246 B.C.E.). The 139/38 B.C.E. letter of the Roman Senate regarding the protection of the Jews (cf. 1 Macc 15:16-24) was also addressed to Cyprus. Judaism in Egypt and Cyprus prospered in particular under Cleopatra III, who during the military conflict with her son Lathyrus (107 B.C.E.) appointed two sons of the high priest Onias IV, who served in exile in Egypt, as commanders in her army.[11] In addition to the Acts of the Apostles, Philo and Josephus also attest to a strong Jewish element in the population of Cyprus in the first century C.E. The island was full of Jewish colonies (Philo, *Leg.* 282). Likewise, Salamis contained numerous synagogues, as Acts 13:5 indicates. Cypriot Jews of this time included two known by name: the magicians Bar-Jesus Elymas (Acts 13:6-8) and Atomos (Joseph., *Ant.* 20.142). Additionally, we know that Alexandria, granddaughter of Herod the Great, married a prominent Cypriot named Timios (*Ant.* 18.131). The great Jewish revolt during the reign of Trajan brought a temporary end to Cypriot Judaism in 115/116 B.C.E. The uprising spread from Alexandria and Cyrene to Cyprus. Under the leadership of a certain Artemion, the Cypriot Jews were said to have

---

contrast, *Acts of Barnabas* 7 states that Barnabas' family lived in a "village" [κώμη] of Cyprus.

[11] Josephus, *Ant.* 13.284-287. Cf. Günther Hölbl, *A History of the Ptolemaic Empire*, trans. Tina Saavedra (London: Routledge, 2001). [Günther Hölbl, *Geschichte des Ptolemäerreiches: Politik, Ideologie und religiöse Kultur von Alexander dem Großen bis zur römischen Eroberung* (Darmstadt: Wissenschaftliche Buchgesellschaft, 1994) 167, 188.]

razed Salamis to the ground and caused the deaths of 240,000 people, leading to a prohibition on the entry of Jews to the island.[12]

Among the Greek deities worshiped in Cyprus,[13] Aphrodite held pride of place. As the island's three most important shrines, the temples of Aphrodite at Palai-Paphos and Amathus, along with the temple of Zeus in Salamis, were granted the traditional right of asylum under Tiberius in 22 C.E. (Tacitus, *Ann.* III 62.4). Strabo refers to additional temples of Aphrodite in Acra and the Pedalium Mountains, as well as a shrine dedicated to both Aphrodite and Isis in Soli (XIV 6.3). Another shrine of Zeus was found in Arsenoe, and an altar to Apollo in Kurion (Strabo XIV 6.3; *Act Barn.* 19).

Significant factors in the economy of Cyprus were mining, exceptionally profitable agriculture—on account of the island's fertility—and finally forestry, which not only made Cyprus an important source of lumber for shipbuilding but also enabled the smelting of copper and silver from the mines.[14]

> Cyprus's fertility exceeds that of any other island. It is rich in wine and oil and produces sufficient grain. There are also rich copper mines near Tamassos, in which copper sulfate is found, as well as verdigris, which is essential for medicinal purposes. Eratosthenes says that in the old days the woods were so vast that one could not cultivate fields, for there were too many trees. Mining has shrunk the forests somewhat, as trees must be felled for the smelting of copper and silver. The outfitting of the fleet has also had an effect, and it sails the sea with courage and power. However, when even this failed to clear sufficient area, they permitted anyone who wished to fell as many trees as he could and then keep the land tax-free as his own (Strabo XIV 6.5).

Commercial trade flourished between Palestine and Cyprus.[15] In 30 B.C.E. Herod the Great received half the income from the copper mines as a gift from Augustus, and the remaining half was entrusted to his

[12] Dio Cassius, *Hist.* LXVIII 32.1-3; Syncellus 1:657. Cf. Emil Schürer and Geza Vermes, *The History of the Jewish People in the Age of Jesus Christ* (Edinburgh: T&T Clark, 1973–87) 1:532; Menachem Stern, *Greek and Latin Authors on Jews and Judaism* (Jerusalem: Israel Academy of Sciences and Humanities, 1980) 2:385–89.

[13] Cf. Terence Bruce Mitford, "The Cults of Roman Cyprus," *ANRW* II 18.3 (1990) 2178–2194.

[14] Cf. Eugen Oberhummer, *Die Insel Cypren: Eine Landeskunde auf historischer Grundlage.* Vol. I: *Quellenkunde und Naturbeschreibung* (Munich: T. Ackermann, 1903) 175–90 (mining); 247–49 (forestry); 270–82 (cultivation of grain); Eugen Oberhummer, "Kypros," *Paulys Realenzyklopädie der klassischen Altertumswissenschaft* (1925) 12:59–117, at 63–74.

[15] Cf. A. Reifenberg, "Das antike zyprische Judentum und seine Beziehungen zu Palästina," *Journal of the Palestine Oriental Society* 12 (1934) 209–15 at 210ff.

administration (Josephus, *Ant.* 16:127-29). When Jerusalem suffered a great famine during the procuracy of Tiberius Alexander (46–48 B.C.E.), Helena, the mother of King Izates of Adiabene, a convert to Judaism, had entire shiploads of figs sent from Cyprus (*Ant.* 20:51, 101). The Talmud offers evidence of the regular Palestinian import of caraway seed from Cyprus *(Qifros)* (*p.Dem.* 2:1 [22b]) and the use of wine from Cyprus *(yen qafrisin)* as an ingredient in the burnt offering on Yom Kippur (*p.Yoma* 4:5 [41d]). This last might indicate that the Jewish community of Cyprus sent an annual gift of wine to the Temple in Jerusalem.[16]

On the basis of this background sketch it is imaginable that Joseph Barnabas was a farmer or merchant dealing in agricultural products, especially if the field he disposed of to benefit the Christian community was in Cyprus. Since in his later career as a Christian missionary he abjured financial support from the local communities and lived by the work of his own hands (1 Cor 9:6), perhaps he, like Paul (Acts 18:3), had been educated in a trade. In any case Joseph Barnabas apparently possessed not inconsiderable wealth and was in this regard not alone in his family. Mary, the mother of his nephew or cousin John Mark (Col 4:10),[17] had a substantial house in Jerusalem with a forecourt and a staff of servants (Acts 12:12-16).

Precisely when Joseph Barnabas made his way from Cyprus to Jerusalem is beyond our knowledge. Little faith can be placed in the assertion that Barnabas was sent to Jerusalem in his youth by his parents in order to study Scripture with Paul under Gamaliel the Elder (Alexander Monachus, *Laudatio* 11.177-81). Most probably Barnabas was one of the many Diaspora Jews who, on account of prosperity gained far from the motherland, had the means to move to Jerusalem—as may have been the case likewise for the Cypriot Jewish Christian Mnason, Paul's host in the city (Acts 21:16). The educational opportunities theoretically available to Joseph Barnabas in Cyprus cannot be clearly determined. The island had played no particular role in intellectual history, even if

[16] Adolf Neubauer, *La Géographie du Talmud* (Paris: Michel Lévy frères, 1868) 369; Oberhummer, *Cypern,* 23.

[17] The meaning of ἀνεψιός (Col 4:10) is analogous to *consobrinus* as used in the Vulgate in its original sense of "nephew" but can be extended to mean "cousin" or "close relative." Cf. Wilhelm Pape, *Griechisch-deutsches Handwörterbuch* (Braunschweig: F. Vieweg und Sohn, 1888) I.1.288. Later legends refer to a brother of Barnabas named Aristoboula, who is said to have been the father-in-law of Simon Peter (Epiphanius Monachus, *Vita Andreae,* Prooemium) and who was both the husband of Mary and the father of John Mark (cf. Lipsius, *Apokryphe Apostelgeschichten,* 342 ff.). For Alexander Monachus, however, Mary is not the sister-in-law but rather the aunt of Barnabas (*Laudatio* 12.202-204).

Zeno, founder of the Stoa, came from Kition (Strabo XIV 6.3). Under Roman rule philosophy and the arts eked out a shadowy existence.[18] At the least Joseph Barnabas, who later worked as a Christian teacher (Acts 11:26; 13:1), possessed an elementary Greek education and a sound knowledge of Scripture.

Levite and Hebrew

In addition to his origins in Cyprus, Acts 4:36 tells us that Joseph Barnabas was a Levite. In principle every member of the tribe of Levi was considered a Levite. More specifically the term referred to someone who performed routine tasks in the Temple. Since the time of Ezekiel (Ezek 44:6-16) the Levites, the lower grade of cultic ministers, had been distinguished from the true priests of Aaronic or, better still, Zadokite lineage. They were permitted to perform only such supportive tasks as guarding the Temple forecourt and slaughtering animals for sacrifice, and they were responsible for singing in the Temple (*Tam.* 7.4).[19] Despite this humble status as *clerus minor,* which they held until shortly before the Jewish War when Agrippa II began to recognize their parity with the Aaronic priesthood (Josephus, *Ant.* 20.216–18), the Levites enjoyed greater prestige than ordinary Israelites.[20] Prominent Levites of the first century c.e. included Jochanan ben Gudhgeda, who served as chief gatekeeper of the Temple (*Shekh.* 2.14; *b.Ar.* 11b), and the respected Scripture scholar Jehoshua ben Chananja, who belonged to the Temple singers (*b.Ar.* 11b). In the case of Barnabas the term Levite probably refers to nothing more than his membership in the tribe of Levi, without implying that he would enter the order of Temple servants.[21] The family of Barnabas, rooted in the Diaspora Judaism of Cyprus, clearly took pride in tracing their genealogy back to the patriarch Levi.

This harmonizes with the statement of Pseudo-Clement that Barnabas was a "Hebrew" (*Hom.* I 9.1; *Recogn.* I 7.7). In contrast to a Hellenist, a

---

[18] Cf. Mitford, "Roman Cyprus," 1365–69.

[19] Cf. Schürer and Vermes, *History,* 2:250–56, 284–87; Joachim Jeremias, *Jerusalem in the Time of Jesus: An Investigation into Economic and Social Conditions During the New Testament Period,* trans. F.H. and C.H. Cave (Philadelphia: Fortress, 1969) 173–81; 207–13; Ulrich Dahmen, "Leviten," *LThK* 6 (1997) 865–67.

[20] Cf. *Qid.* 4.1; *Git.* 5.8; *b.Git.* 59b; R. Meyer, "Λευ(ε)ίτης," *TDNT* 4 (1942) 239–41.

[21] A different view regarding the education of Barnabas is given by Ludger Schenke, *Die Urgemeinde: Geschichtliche und theologische Entwicklung* (Stuttgart: Kohlhammer, 1990), with far-reaching consequences: "He [Barnabas] had good command of Hebrew/Aramaic on account of his work in service to the Temple. . . . As a Levite, he possessed a theological education. He had mastered Holy Scripture and the early Jewish tradition" (79–80).

Hebrew who was not himself from Palestine was a Diaspora Jew who had mastered Hebrew or Aramaic and felt close ties to the Palestinian motherland.[22] This characterization applies to Barnabas, who through Mary, the mother of his nephew or cousin John Mark, had family connections to Jerusalem (Acts 12:12; Col 4:10).

---

[22] Martin Hengel, "Der vorchristliche Paulus," in Martin Hengel and Ulrich Heckel, eds., *Paulus und das antike Judentum* (Tübingen: J.C.B. Mohr [Paul Siebeck], 1991) 220–22.

Barnabas in the
Early Christian Community

The "Conversion" of Barnabas

A "conversion" of Barnabas was first reported by Alexander Monachus, whose account stated that Barnabas became a follower of Jesus as a result of the healing of a lame man (John 5:2-9) and other miracles in the Temple (Matt 21:14). In the New Testament, however, Barnabas makes his first appearance in Acts 4:36 with the sale of his field and from then on occupies a prominent position in the Christian community of Jerusalem. How long he had belonged to the community prior to this point and whether he had known the historical Jesus remain unclear.

The early church showed a pronounced interest in connecting Barnabas as closely as possible to Jesus. At the end of the second century C.E. at the latest he was being included among the seventy or seventy-two sent out by Jesus in Luke 10:1.[1] Barnabas was subsequently identified with Matthias, who was chosen to take the place of Judas in the group of twelve apostles.[2] Since Barnabas, as a Diaspora Jew, may have been resident in Jerusalem for an extended period of time, one ought to consider whether he perhaps at least encountered Jesus. However, if one accepts the synoptic chronology, which includes but a single visit to

---

[1] Clement of Alexandria, *Stromateis* II 116.3; Eusebius, *Hist. Eccl.* I 12.1; II 1.4; Epiphanius, *De incarnatione* 4.4 (*Panarion* XX); cf. Theodor Schermann, *Propheten- und Apostellegenden nebst Jüngerkatalogen des Dorotheus und verwandter Texte* (Leipzig: J.C. Hinrichs, 1907) 292–321. In *Ps.-Clem. Hom.* I 9.1; *Recogn.* I 7.7 as well Barnabas appears during Jesus' lifetime as one of his disciples. On the basis of this Adolf von Harnack, in *The Mission and Expansion of Christianity in the First Three Centuries,* trans. James Moffatt (New York: G.P. Putnam's Sons, 1908) 1:52 n. 1, noted that Barnabas "belongs from the very beginning to the church of Jerusalem (perhaps he was a follower of Jesus)."

[2] *Ps.-Clem. Recogn.* I 60.5 ("Barnabas, who is also called Matthias, who was chosen as an apostle to take the place of Judas").

Jerusalem by Jesus, such an encounter could only have taken place during the Passover before Jesus' death in the year 30 C.E. and, given that the city would have been overrun with pilgrims during this festival season, it must be deemed highly unlikely.

One can with greater plausibility assume that Barnabas joined Jesus' followers after Easter and, furthermore, likely did so because he experienced an epiphany. On the basis of the arguments put forth in 1 Cor 9:4-6 it is clear that Paul himself, as well as the Corinthians, considered Barnabas an apostle.[3] Otherwise the authoritative appeal to Barnabas—whose missionary style, like Paul's, was characterized by his refusal to accept the support he was due from the local community—would provide no conclusive evidence of the legitimacy of the Pauline apostolate. For Paul the apostolate is founded entirely upon the epiphany of his encounter with the risen Lord (1 Cor 9:1; 15:8-10). Consequently, when Paul speaks of Barnabas as an apostle this presumes that Barnabas also experienced a vision of Christ,[4] and Paul either included him among that majority of the five hundred brothers and sisters mentioned in 1 Cor 15:6 who were still alive or, more likely, considered him one of "all the apostles" referred to in 15:7. These relatively reliable accounts provide a basis for the consideration of additional questions. The appearance before the five hundred may be related to the Pentecost event of Acts 2:1-13 since such a dramatic occurrence, most of whose participants were still alive in the fifties C.E. and could provide eyewitness accounts, would certainly merit some mention in the Acts of the Apostles, and John 20:22 also refers to an epiphany of the risen Lord, who imparts the Holy Spirit to the disciples.[5] According to Acts 2:5 Diaspora Jews who had returned to Jerusalem witnessed the miracle of Pentecost, which historically consisted in the Spirit-granted glossolalia of the participants (Acts 2:4). Even though Cypriot Jews are not mentioned in the list of peoples in Acts 2:9-11—which was, in any case, added to the

[3] Cf. Walter Schmithals, *The Office of Apostle in the Early Church,* trans. John E. Steely (Nashville: Abingdon, 1969) 63–67; Wolf-Henning Ollrog, *Paulus und seine Mitarbeiter: Untersuchungen zu Theorie und Praxis der paulinischen Mission* (Neukirchen-Vluyn: Neukirchener Verlag, 1979) 16.

[4] Christian Wolff, *Der erste Brief des Paulus an die Korinther* (Berlin: Evangelische Verlagsanstalt, 1990) 2:21: "For Paul, apostles were [those] who had received a special mission of proclamation from the Risen Lord."

[5] Regarding the possible identity of the appearance before the five hundred with the Pentecost event cf. Gerd Lüdemann, *The Resurrection of Jesus: History, Experience, Theology,* trans. John Bowden (London: S.C.M., 1994) 100–106. The most significant counterarguments can be found in, e.g., Jacob Kremer, *Pfingstbericht und Pfingstgeschehen: Eine exegetische Untersuchung zu Apg 2, 1-13* (Stuttgart: KBW Verlag, 1973) 232–37.

account by Luke to support the new interpretation of the Pentecost event as a miracle of speaking in tongues—Barnabas may have been inspired to follow Jesus on account of witnessing the Pentecost miracle and had in this context a vision of the risen Christ (1 Cor 15:6-7).

Renunciation of Possessions for the Benefit of the Community

Luke derived his portrayal of early Christian communal living in love found in Acts 2:42-27 and 4:32-35 from the story of Joseph Barnabas' surrender of his possessions (4:36-37).[6]

That Barnabas sold a field belonging to him and put the proceeds at the disposal of the Christian community of Jerusalem is beyond doubt. Less clear, however, is the question of whether it was a parcel of land purchased or inherited *in Jerusalem*.[7] Alternatively, Barnabas may have sold the field in Cyprus,[8] perhaps only shortly before he moved to Jerusalem. It is in no way necessary to assume that the sale of the field occurred only after the Council of Jerusalem on account of the arrangements made there to take up a collection and that Luke projected the event back onto the beginnings of the church.[9]

Within the early Christian community Barnabas' sale of the field represented a particularly memorable act of charity,[10] although it was not an entirely singular event. Ananias and Sapphira had likewise sold a piece of property for the benefit of the Christian community, though they retained part of the proceeds (Acts 5:1-11). While those disciples of Jesus who came from rural Galilee had abandoned their not inconsiderable property upon becoming his followers (Mark 10:28) and were thus deprived of the very basis of their existence, there were in the

[6] Alfons Weiser, *Die Apostelgeschichte* (Gütersloh: Gerd Mohn, 1981/1985) 1:137: "The concisely narrated example of the sale of the field by Joseph Barnabas appears to be the traditional historical kernel of the preceding statement about communal ownership."

[7] Gerhard Schneider, *Die Apostelgeschichte* (Freiburg: Herder, 1980/1982) 1:367: "Barnabas—as a Diaspora Jew resident in Jerusalem—possessed a field (in the area around the city)."

[8] Cf. Rudolf Pesch, *Die Apostelgeschichte* (Zurich: Neukirchener Verlag, 1986) 1:183–84.

[9] Gerd Lüdemann, *Early Christianity According to the Traditions in Acts: A Commentary,* trans. John Bowden (Minneapolis: Fortress, 1989) 62–63. A similar position is taken by Walter Schmithals, *Die Apostelgeschichte des Lukas* (Zurich: Theologischer Verlag, 1982) 54, who combines this with the groundless speculation, also put forth by Gottfried Schille, *Die Apostelgeschichte des Lukas* (Berlin: Evangelische Verlagsanstalt, 1989), that Barnabas was never part of the original Christian community but rather was first included in it by Luke.

[10] Weiser, *Die Apostelgeschichte,* 1:138: "The fact that Barnabas' charitable act was remembered reveals it as an exception and not simply the usual behavior of everyone, entirely apart from the fact that there would not have been many wealthy Christians in the primitive community."

Greek-speaking circles of the Christian community returnees from the Diaspora who had in the past achieved a certain affluence and who shared their wealth with poorer members of the community. "The most important donor, who enabled the dream of such a solidarity born of equality, was the Hellenist Barnabas of Cyprus."[11] The generalized Lukan reports of a renunciation of property both obligatory and comprehensive are not, however, covered by the underlying traditions and owe their existence instead to a transfigured portrayal of the life of the Christian community of Jerusalem, influenced by Pythagorean-Essene ideals of an organized communal holding of property.

In the initiation ritual of the Pythagoreans (Iamblichus, *Vit. Pyth.* 17:72-74), as well as of the Essenes (Philo, *Hyp.* 11:4; Josephus, *Bell.* II:122, 124-127), complete alienation of private property, or rather the handing over of the property for communal ownership, was firmly institutionalized. In the case of the Qumran Essenes this is proven by 1 QS VI:19-20, as well as by an ostracon discovered in 1996. The clay fragment records that a certain Honi from Jerusalem, evidently a novice, fulfilled his oath by handing over his possessions to Eleazar, who must have had charge of the property of the Qumran community.[12]

The historical basis of the early Christian community's communal sharing of property was a form of renunciation of possessions based on free will (Acts 5:4) and, due to anticipation of the imminent return of Christ, was not carefully organized or administered. This is manifested on the one hand in the socialization of private property, as when, for example, houses were given to the community to be used for communal worship services (Acts 2:46; 12:12-17), and on the other hand in the selling of property and placing the proceeds at the disposal of the community (Acts 4:37; 5:1-11). Barnabas' selling of the field, as significant as it was, ought thus to be understood not as a complete surrender of property but rather as a partial disposal of that property for charitable reasons.[13]

---

[11] Gerd Theissen, "Hellenisten und Hebräer (Apg 6:1-6): Gab es eine Spaltung in der Urgemeinde?" in Hermann Lichtenberger, ed., *Geschichte—Tradition—Reflexion* (Tübingen: J.C.B. Mohr [Paul Siebeck], 1996) 339.

[12] Edition and commentary by Frank Moore Cross and Esther Eschel, "Ostraca from Khirbet Qumrân," *Israel Exploration Journal* 47 (1997) 17–28. Cf. also Hans-Josef Klauck, "Gütergemeinschaft in der klassischen Antike, in Qumran und im Neuen Testament," *Revue de Qumran* 11 (1982) 47–79.

[13] Cf. the rabbinic parallel *LevR* V,3 (ed. A. Wünsche), in which Abba Judan sells half of his field for charitable purposes.

The Name Barnabas

According to Acts 4:36, the Levite Joseph was first given the additional name Barnabas, meaning "son of encouragement" (υἱὸς παρα-κλήσεως), by the Jerusalem apostles. The conjecture that, contrary to the account of the "artificial giving" of this second name found in Acts 4:36, he had "as a Hellenistic Jew always had this name in addition to his Jewish name Joseph,"[14] is implausible since Barnabas is a *Semitic* name.[15]

Etymologically the name Barnabas, unknown outside the New Testament, presents considerable problems, including its purported definition, "son of encouragement." While *bar* is obviously traceable to the Aramaic בַּר (son), it is unclear from which Semitic word the second part of the name, *nabas,* derives. Barnabas is occasionally considered a version of *bar nebuah* ("son of prophecy"),[16] but this is not synonymous with "son of encouragement." A leap must be made to reach the next etymologically related name, *bar nebu,* son of Nabu, a Palmyran proper name, rendered in Greek as Βαρνεβοῦς and appearing in Latin documents as *Barnebus.*[17] Either the translation of Barnabas as "son of encouragement" represents an inaccurate popular etymology[18] or "son of encouragement" originally referred to Manaen (Acts 13:1), the Greek form of Menachem ("the encourager") and was incorrectly applied by Luke to Barnabas.[19]

It is, however, scarcely imaginable that the Jerusalem apostles would *consciously* refer to the Levite Joseph as son of the heathen deity Nabu. By use of the appellation Barnabas, the Cypriot Levite Joseph was distinguishable from others in the Christian community who bore that name, in particular that Joseph who was considered as a successor to Judas and who went by the additional names Barsabbas and Justus (Acts 1:23). It is possible that the choice of name also represents a play on words, in that the community placed a Joseph Barnabas beside the

[14] Schmithals, *Die Apostelgeschichte,* 54.

[15] For this reason the two-part name Joseph Barnabas is not directly comparable to the Semitic-Latin double names of such Hellenistic Jews as Saul-Paul, John Mark, or Silas-Silvanus. This is confirmed by the fact that Joseph Barsabbas (Acts 1:23) used the additional Latin name Justus as well. Presumably Joseph Barnabas, as a Diaspora Jew, had an additional Latin or Greek name that has not been preserved.

[16] (Herman Leberecht Strack and) Paul Billerbeck, *Kommentar zum Neuen Testament aus Talmud und Midrasch* (Munich: Beck, 1922–1928) 2:634; Weiser, *Die Apostelgeschichte,* 1:138.

[17] Fundamental on this topic are Gustav Adolf Deissmann, *Bible Studies,* trans. Alexander Grieve (Edinburgh: T & T Clark, 1901) 188, 309. Cf. also Hans Peter Rüger, "Aramäisch II. Im Neuen Testament," *TRE* (1978) 599–610, at 604.

[18] Cf. Sebastian Brock, "ΒΑΡΝΑΒΑΣ· ΥΙΟΣ ΠΑΡΑΚΛΗΣΕΩΣ," *JTS* 25 (1974) 93–98.

[19] Cf. Ernst Haenchen, *The Acts of the Apostles: A Commentary,* trans. Bernard Noble and Gerald Shinn (Oxford: Blackwell, 1971) 232.

Joseph Barsabbas of Acts 1:23 without being aware of the original heathen significance of this Greek Semitic proper name.

Barnabas and the Stephen Group

On account of the sale of his field, discussed above, Barnabas assumed a prominent position in the early Christian community even
though he was included in neither the Twelve (Acts 1:13) nor the Seven
(Acts 6:5), its two leading groups. Perhaps he was already active as a
teacher, as was unquestionably the case later in Antioch (Acts 11:26).
On the basis of family connections (Col 4:10), Barnabas belonged to the
household of Mary, the mother of John Mark. Her substantial house in
Jerusalem served as a gathering place for Greek-speaking members of
the Christian community, undoubtedly including Peter (Acts 12:12-
27).[20] His theological profile indicates that Barnabas was probably associated intellectually with the Hellenists of Stephen's circle.

On the basis of the Acts of the Apostles the contours of the descrip-
tions "Hebrew" and "Hellenist" in the early Christian community (Acts
6:1) can be determined only in outline. According to Luke—who was
the first to use this term and apparently employed it in an *ad hoc* fash-
ion without reliance on an earlier tradition—Hellenists are Greek-
speaking Jews of Jerusalem (Acts 6:1; 9:29), without implying anything
regarding membership in the Christian community or any particular
theological position on such matters as the Law.[21] The particular position of those Hellenists in the circle of Stephen, however, was in conti-
nuity with the central ideas of Jesus' preaching[22] and was characterized
by a questioning of certain teachings of the Mosaic Torah (Acts 6:11)
and a critical view of the Temple cult (6:13-14). They clearly attached a
secondary significance to parts of the Jewish ritual law and were per-

[20] Cf. Hans-Josef Klauck, *Hausgemeinde und Hauskirche im frühen Christentum* (Stuttgart:
Katholisches Bibelwerk, 1981) 48–51; Elisabeth Schlüssler Fiorenza, *In Memory of Her: A
Feminist Theological Reconstruction of Christian Origins* (New York: Crossroad, 1983) 163–67.

[21] Cf. Martin Hengel, "Zwischen Jesus und Paulus: Die 'Hellenisten,' die 'Sieben' und
Stephanus (Apg 6:1-15; 7:54-8:3)," *ZTK* 72 (1975) 160–68. If in Acts 11:20 Ἑλληνιστάς is
the original version (see below), then Luke subsumes under "Hellenists" Greek-speaking
Jews as well as Greek-speaking Gentiles. Cf. Wolfgang Reinbold, "Die 'Hellenisten': Kritische Anmerkungen zu einem Fachbegriff der neutestamentlichen Wissenschaft," *BZ* 42
(1998) 97–99, who incidentally rightly cautions against understanding under "Hellenists" a strictly defined intra-church group with specific theological views (99–102).

[22] François Vouga, *Geschichte des frühen Christentums* (Tübingen: Francke, 1994) 40–46,
even speculates that the Hellenists of the early Christian community were, as Passover
pilgrims, witnesses to the Jerusalem deeds of Jesus.

haps beginning to adopt an interpretation of Jesus' death as an expiatory sacrifice (cf. Rom 3:25), which qualified the Temple's function as the place of sacrifice.[23] Thus they attracted the enmity of other Hellenists—namely those Greek-speaking Diaspora Jews who had returned to Jerusalem from foreign parts not least on account of the Torah and the Temple—leading to the martyrdom of Stephen and the expulsion of his followers (cf. Acts 9:29). Likewise, despite their shared absolute observance of the Law, the "Hebrews" did not represent a homogeneous party within the Christian community. In the midst of their ranks stood the Lord's brother James, who was called "the Righteous," primarily on account of his impeccable adherence to the Law (*GThom* Logion 12; Eusebius *Hist. Eccl.* II 23.4-7). To the right of James stood an influential faction of Pharisaic members of the community (Acts 15:5; 21:20-24; Gal 2:4), characterized by an especially rigorous attitude toward the Law. On the opposite side Simon Peter, an erstwhile leader of the Hebrews later superseded by James, initiated contact with the Hellenistic household of Mary, which perhaps, like Stephen and his circle, criticized the ritual laws (Acts 12:12-17), and emerged as a representative of the movement in the early Church toward liberalizing observance of the Law (Acts 10:1-48; 11:3; Gal 2:12).

As a Greek-speaking Diaspora Jew who as a "Hebrew" knew the language of the motherland and felt a close connection to Palestine, Barnabas effectively straddled the line dividing Hellenist and Hebrew. He surely had an important mediating function between these two factions of the early Christian community[24] with regard not only to language but also—at least as far as relations between the Hebrews and the Hellenists of Stephen's circle were concerned—to substantive disagreements. To reach a more precise definition of Barnabas' theological position it is necessary to consider that a few years after the martyrdom of Stephen he played a leading role (Acts 13:1) in the Christian community of Antioch

[23] For such a legalistic understanding of Stephen's circle with differing emphases cf. Hengel, "Zwischen Jesus und Paulus," 186–96; Ludger Schenke, *Die Urgemeinde: Geschichtliche und theologische Entwicklung* (Stuttgart: Kohlhammer, 1990) 176–85; Heikki Räisänen, "Die 'Hellenisten' der Urgemeinde," 1482–91; Gerd Theissen, "Hellenisten und Hebräer," 332–38. For a critical view see Eckhard Rau, *Von Jesus zu Paulus: Entwicklung und Rezeption der antio-chenischen Theologie im Urchristentum* (Stuttgart: Kohlhammer, 1994) 15–77: nothing indicates that the Hellenists were critical of the Law; Klaus Haaker, "Die Stellung des Stephanus in der Geschichte des Urchristentums," *ANRW* II 26,2 (1995) 1515–53: the accusations of Acts 6:11, 13-14 are not to be taken at face value; Stephen in no way questioned the sacred values (Torah and Temple) of Judaism, but rather attracted malicious aggression on account of "intellectual superiority" (1547).

[24] Schenke, *Urgemeinde,* 79; Räisänen, "Hellenisten," 1478.

with its mission to the Gentiles, who were no longer obligated to undergo circumcision (Acts 11:20), and he chose, in the person of Paul, a companion who considered himself specially elected as the apostle to the Gentiles (Gal 1:15-24). This clearly indicates that in terms of theology Barnabas—who probably stood not far from Peter as a representative of the "left wing" of the Hebrews—ought to be placed quite close to Stephen and his circle, rather than in the immediate vicinity of the strictly observant Hebrews.[25]

Important evidence indicates that Barnabas was among those men from Cyprus and Cyrene who, as a result of Stephen's martyrdom, went from Jerusalem to Antioch and there for the first time began to carry out the planned mission to the Gentiles. However, the historical account presented in the Acts of the Apostles, which is now being questioned, contradicts this theory, as it states that Barnabas remained in Jerusalem even about three years after the demise of Stephen's circle (9:26-30) and only later was sent by the Christian community to Antioch as their "missionary to Syria" (11:22).

Mediator between Paul and the Apostles?

According to Luke's account (Acts 9:26-30) Barnabas dispelled the Jerusalem community's reservations about Paul and paved the way for the onetime persecutor of Christians to become their advocate. "But Barnabas took him, brought him to the apostles, and he (i.e., Barnabas)[26] told them how he (i.e., Paul) had seen the Lord on the road and spoken with him and how he had gone about in Damascus, boldly speaking the name of Jesus. And he went in and out among them in Jerusalem" (Acts 9:27-28).[27] This arrival of Paul in Jerusalem must correspond to the fifteen-day visit to Cephas, mentioned by Paul in Gal 1:1-18, that took place three years after the Damascus experience. For Luke the apostles of Acts 9:27 are identical to the circle of the Twelve, with whom Paul subsequently spent his time in Jerusalem, thanks to the personal

[25] In contrast, Martin Hengel, *Acts and the History of Earliest Christianity,* trans. John Bowden (Philadelphia: Fortress, 1980) 101–102, confirms that Barnabas was "closely in touch with the freer Greek-speaking communities," but does not doubt "that the Levite from Cyprus was originally one of the core community in Jerusalem directed by the 'Twelve' (Acts 4:36; 9:27), i.e., was one of the 'Hebrews.'"

[26] The majority of commentators concur. Theoretically, however, a change in subject between Barnabas and Paul is debatable.

[27] Editor's note: The author's interpretation of the passage contradicts the translation of the NRSV, which therefore is not used here. NRSV takes "he" as referring to Paul, not to Barnabas.

advocacy of Barnabas. Paul himself freely acknowledged that, besides Cephas and James, he knew none of the apostles, and he even swore to this (Gal 1:20) in order to demonstrate for the Galatian community his independence from the Jerusalem authorities. Since Paul considered the Twelve to be apostles, on account of their Easter vision (1 Cor 15:4), and also included Barnabas in their ranks (1 Cor 9:5-6), it can be concluded on the basis of Gal 1:1-18 that at the time he had met neither any member of the Twelve besides Cephas[28] nor Barnabas. This is further indicated by his statement during his later journeys to Syria and Cilicia that he remained personally unknown to the churches of Judea and thus to large parts of the Christian community.

The purported mediating role of Barnabas, plausible as it may seem at first glance, is ruled out by Gal 1:18-20, if Paul is taken at his word.[29] With Acts 9:26-30 Luke intended to show that Paul stood in harmony with the Twelve soon after his conversion, and he clearly excluded the mediating role of Barnabas in favor of that of Paul in his accounts of their later work in Antioch.

---

[28] James, the Lord's brother, the only apostle besides Cephas whom Paul met (Gal 1:19), was not considered an apostle by Luke because he did not belong to the Twelve and thus cannot be concealed behind the apostles of Acts 9:27.

[29] A different position is held by Martin Hengel, "Die Stellung des Apostels Paulus zum Gesetz in den unbekannten Jahren zwischen Damaskus und Antiochen," in James D.G. Dunn, ed., *Paul and the Mosaic Law* (Tübingen: J.C.B. Mohr [Paul Siebeck], 1996) 39: In Gal 1:19 Paul meant the *Jerusalem* apostles and did not include Barnabas among them. For a similar view see Christoph Burchard, *Der dreizehnte Zeuge: Traditions- und kompositionsgeschichtliche Untersuchungen zu Lukas' Darstellung der Frühzeit des Paulus* (Göttingen: Vandenhoeck & Ruprecht, 1970) 160 n. 107.

Barnabas in Antioch

The City of Antioch

Barnabas traveled from Jerusalem to Antioch to assume a position of leadership in the Christian community there. Since 64 B.C.E. Antioch on the Orontes had been the capital of the Roman province of Syria and was, after Rome and Alexandria, the third-largest city in the Roman empire. Estimates of Antioch's population, which can be inferred from ancient texts, vary from 200,000 to 600,000, depending on how slaves and inhabitants of the suburbs are counted.[1] Presumably in the New Testament period the total population encompassed some 500,000 people.

In addition to the long-established Syrian population, large numbers of Macedonians, Greeks, and Jews made their home in ancient Antioch (Josephus, *Ant.* XII, 119). Given that approximately thirteen per cent of the provincial population of Syria was Jewish, Antioch likely had about 65,000 Jewish inhabitants and numerous synagogues.[2] According to Josephus the origins of the Jewish community could be traced back to the days of the Seleucid kings and the city's founder, Seleukos I Nikator (312–280 B.C.E.). This ruler guaranteed rights of citizenship for the Jews (*Ant.* XII, 119), and as Antiochenes they enjoyed equal status with the rest of the city's citizens (Josephus, *Ap.* II, 39). When Titus visited Antioch in 70 C.E. these privileges granted the Jews were still inscribed on bronze tablets (Josephus, *Bell.* VII, 110).

The Judaism of Antioch, which prospered on account of the rights granted it, held a particular appeal for the surrounding Gentile community. "They adorned their shrine with rich and elaborate offerings

---

[1] Cf. Frederick W. Norris, "Antiochien I. Neutestamentlich," *TRE* 3 (1978) 99–103, at 99.

[2] Cf. Carl H. Kraeling, "The Jewish Community at Antioch," *JBL* 51 (1932) 130–60, at 135–41; additionally, Wayne Meeks and Robert L. Wilken, *Jews and Christians in Antioch in the First Four Centuries of the Common Era* (Missoula: Scholars, 1978) 2–13.

and continually induced many Greeks to attend their worship services, making them in a way a part of their community" (*Bell.* VII, 45). We encounter here the phenomenon of the God-fearers. Greek men and, above all, Greek women, including many members of the upper class, were attracted by monotheism and the ethics of Judaism. They acted as *sebomenoi* or *phoboumenoi* in association with the synagogue, without taking upon themselves the whole of the Torah or becoming proselytes.[3] Admittedly, the religious landscape of Antioch was dominated by the temples of nearly all the classical Greek deities, including the particularly renowned shrine of Apollo in the suburb of Daphne.[4]

The Origins of the Christian Community in Antioch

Acts 11:19-26 provides some details of the founding of the Christian community in Antioch. Of particular significance is the fact that the Jerusalem Hellenist Nicholas, a member of Stephen's circle, was a proselyte from Antioch (Acts 6:5). Although we have no reliable information about Nicholas' fate after Stephen's martyrdom,[5] he may have returned to his native city of Antioch with other persecuted followers of Stephen (Acts 11:19). In any case, it was on account of the scattering of Stephen's circle from Jerusalem that, only a few years after Jesus' death, the originally rural Jesus movement gained a foothold in the third-largest city of the Roman empire, with its considerable Macedonian and Greek populations, and began to take on an urban character. A

[3] Regarding the question of the God-fearers see the summary of research in Bernd Wander, *Trennungsprozesse zwischen Frühen Christentum und Judentum im 1. Jahrhundert n.Chr.: Datierbare Abfolgen zwischen der Hinrichtung Jesu und der Zerstörung des Jerusalemer Tempels* (Tübingen: Francke, 1994) 173–85.

[4] Regarding primarily those Hellenistic cults in ancient Antioch attested by the Chronicle of Malalas (6th c. B.C.E.), cf. Alexander Schenk Graf von Stauffenberg, *Die römische Kaisergeschichte bei Malalas: Griechischer Text der Bücher IX–XII und Untersuchungen* (Stuttgart: Kohlhammer, 1931) 444–92; Frederick W. Norris, "Antioch-on-the-Orontes as a Religious Center, I: Paganism before Constantine," *ANRW* II 18.4 (1990) 2322–79; on archaeological findings see Jean Lassus, "La ville d'Antioche à l'époque romaine d'après l'archéologie," *ANRW* II 8 (1977) 54–102; on the overall religious landscape of ancient Syria see Andreas Feldtkeller, *Im Reich der Syrischen Göttin: Eine religiös plurale Kultur als Umwelt des frühen Christentums* (Gütersloh: Gütersloher Verlagshaus, 1994).

[5] A reflection of his overt antinomianism is provided by the ecclesiastical tradition of Nicholas as founder of the Nicolaitans (Rev 2:6, 15; Irenaeus, *Haer.* I 26.5; Eusebius, *Hist. Eccl.* III 29.1), who approved the eating of meat that had been offered to idols. Cf. Roman Heiligenthal, "Wer waren die 'Nikolaiten'?: Ein Beitrag zur Theologiegeschichte des frühen Christentums," *ZNW* 82 (1991) 133–37; Heikki Räisänen, "The Nicolaitans: Apoc. 2; Acta 6," *ANRW* II 26.2 (1995) 1602–44.

decisive factor was that some of Stephen's followers who went to Antioch began a direct mission to the Gentiles without establishing ties to the synagogue. "But there were a few men among them from Cyprus and Cyrene who, upon arriving in Antioch, spoke also to the Greeks[6] and proclaimed the Lord Jesus" (Acts 11:20). This statement is based on a pre-Lukan tradition. That members of Stephen's circle were the first to carry out an organized mission to the Gentiles is in tension with Luke's interest in portraying Peter as the founder of that mission (Acts 10:1-48). The potential for the Antiochene mission to the Gentiles may have been found, at least early on, in the circles of the God-fearers, mentioned by Josephus (*Bell.* VII.45), but adherents of Antioch's countless Hellenistic cults were also soon won for Christianity.

The pre-Lukan tradition included in Acts 11:20 mentions unnamed "men from Cyprus and Cyrene" as protagonists in the mission directed specifically at the Gentiles, and the likewise pre-Lukan list of names in Acts 13:1, which places the Cypriot Barnabas first, includes a Lucius of Cyrene, followed by Simeon Niger, also of Cyrene, whose name may indicate African origins. In contrast to the Lukan theory of Barnabas as the "Syrian nuncio"[7] of the early Christian community (11:22), these two ancient traditions of Acts 11:20 and 13:1, presumably of Antiochene origin, taken together suggest that Barnabas, Lucius, and even Simeon Niger were among those Cypriots and Cyrenians who first carried out an organized mission to the Gentiles in Antioch.[8] Consequently, Barnabas would have been "one of those men of the early Christian community who, presumably along with other members of Stephen's circle, inaugurated the mission to the Gentiles, that is, one of those dispersed from Jerusalem by persecution who then founded the Antiochene

---

[6] Ἕλληνας (𝔓[74], ℵ[c], A, D*) may take precedence over the *lectio difficilior* Ἑλληνιστάς (B, D[c], ψ, 1739, 𝔐) favored by Nestle-Aland (cf., e.g., Wolfgang Reinbold, "Die 'Hellenisten': Kritische Anmerkungen zu einem Fachbegriff der neutestamentlichen Wissenschaft," *BZ* 42 (1998) 96–102). For overall coherence, Greek-speaking *Gentiles* rather than Jews (in Antioch also Greek speakers) (11:19) must be intended. In case Ἑλληνιστάς is original, it may be understood as a specification of the Greek-speaking "Macedonians and Hellenes" of Antioch (Josephus, *Ant.* XII.119; *Bell.* VII.45) as opposed to the established Syrian populace of the city.

[7] Characterization of the historical Barnabas by Heinrich Schlier, *Der Brief an die Galater* (Göttingen: Vandenhoeck & Ruprecht, 1971) 5. Opposing this position is Acts 11:22, which reveals the typical Lukan desire to bind newly founded congregations immediately to the apostolic center at Jerusalem.

[8] Ernst Haenchen, *The Acts of the Apostles: A Commentary,* trans. Bernard Noble and Gerald Shinn (Oxford: Blackwell, 1971) 365–67.

Christian community."[9] Alternatively, as a "partial" sympathizer with
Stephen's circle, Barnabas may have followed on the heels of the other
Hellenists but been impelled purely by personal theological conviction
rather than by the pressures of persecution.

Acts 11:19-26 does not indicate to what extent the authority of the
Torah was set aside for those Antiochene Gentiles who converted to belief in *Kyrios Iesous*. In any case, the newly won Gentiles were not circumcised (cf. Gal 2:3; Acts 15:5). In this regard three formulations from
the Pauline letters merit attention, as they presumably address traditions of the Antiochene Christian community[10] that serve to legitimate
the rejection of circumcision:

- Circumcision is nothing, and uncircumcision is nothing, but obedience to the commandments of God is everything (1 Cor 7:19).
- For in Christ Jesus neither circumcision nor uncircumcision means
  anything, but rather faith working through love (Gal 5:6).
- For neither circumcision nor uncircumcision is anything, but a
  new creation is everything (Gal 6:15).

Although the specific wording varies, a strikingly similar two-part
structure underlies all three of these statements. First, any distinction in
status between the circumcised and the uncircumcised is declared mean-
ingless,[11] while at the same time a distinctive Christian concept is put
forth as eminently meaningful. While in Gal 6:15 this concept is the new
creation, 1 Cor 7:19 and Gal 5:6 present a new ethical-juridical requirement in which circumcision as a sign of "obedience to the law of God" is
renounced in favor of faith working through love. In reality this necessi-
tated setting aside the Torah's requirement of male circumcision, which

[9] Wolfgang Schrage, *Der erste Brief an die Korinther* (Neukirchen-Vluyn: Neukirchener
Verlag, 1995) 2:295. Similarly, Wilhelm Schneemelcher, *Das Urchristentum* (Stuttgart:
Kohlhammer, 1981) 128, considers Barnabas the founder of the Antiochene congregation,
on the basis of Acts 13:1.

[10] Regarding the stereotypical character and presumable Antiochene origin of 1 Cor
7:19; Gal 5:6; and Gal 6:15 cf. Ulrich Mell, *Neue Schöpfung: Eine traditionsgeschichtliche und
exegetische Studie zu einem soteriologischen Grundsatz paulinischer Theologie* (Berlin and New
York: Walter de Gruyter, 1989) 298–302; Eckhard Rau, *Von Jesus zu Paulus: Entwicklung und
Rezeption der antiochenischen Theologie im Urchristentum* (Stuttgart: Kohlhammer, 1994)
86–96; Friedrich Wilhelm Horn, "Der Verzicht auf die Beschneidung im frühen Christentum," *NTS* 42 (1996) 484–86, 495–97.

[11] Presumably in the background is the pre-Pauline tradition of 1 Cor 12:13 and Gal
3:26-28 with its declaration of the abolition of the distinction between Jews and Greeks by
virtue of baptism in Christ. Cf. Jürgen Becker, *Paul, Apostle to the Gentiles*, trans. O. C. Dean,
Jr. (Louisville: Westminster John Knox, 1993) 104–12; Rau, *Von Jesus zu Paulus*, 86–90.

led inexorably to rejection of the ceremonial laws embodied in circumcision in favor of a moral law centered on the commandment of love.[12] This background also makes clear why, in addition to circumcision, the Jewish dietary laws had lost their authoritative force in the Christian community of Antioch by the time of the Antiochene crisis at the latest (Gal 2:11-14).

Because in Antioch the community brought together by a shared faith in *Kyrios Iesous* encompassed for the first time a significant number of people who had not first been proselytes, the name "Christian" (Χριστιανοί) arose there (Acts 11:26). This did not yet imply a separation of the church from Judaism,[13] but it began paving the way toward such separation through a growing self-awareness over against the synagogue. As long as the followers of Jesus remained faithful to the Torah in its entirety they represented a party within the synagogue—the Nazarenes (Acts 24:5) or *Nosrim (Shemoneh Esreh)*—as was the case for the Christian community of Jerusalem until the Jewish War. Antioch, on the other hand, could be characterized *cum grano salis* as the cradle of Christianity since the community there, consisting of both baptized Jews and Gentiles who had given up observing some parts of the Torah, no longer went to the synagogue and could also be distinguished from the Jewish community by their name, "Christians." This was an unfamiliar term that in the end gained rapid acceptance among Gentile writers.[14] Significantly, we encounter the common self-description *Xristianoi* in the Didache, which had Syrian origins (12:4), and in Ignatius of Antioch (*IgnEph* 11:2; *IgnMagn* 4; *IgnRom* 3:2).[15]

[12] For possible links with the Antiochene renunciation of male circumcision, especially the Hellenistic-Jewish understanding of circumcision as a purely symbolic cutting off of lust and desire—a position refuted by Philo, *Migr.* 89–93—see Rau, *Von Jesus zu Paulus,* 96–100; Klaus Berger, *Theologie des Urchristentums: Theologie des Neuen Testaments* (Tübingen: Francke, 1995) 282–86; Horn, "Verzicht auf die Beschneidung," 490–95.

[13] Cf. Wander, *Trennungsprozesse,* 193–95; Helga Botermann, *Das Judenedikt des Kaisers Claudius: Römischer Staat und Christiani im 1. Jahrhundert* (Stuttgart: Steiner, 1996) 157–67; Klaus Haacker, "Zum Werdegang des Apostels Paulus: Biographische Daten und ihre theologische Relevanz," *ANRW* II 26.2 (1995), 815–938, 1924–33, at 924–25, all of whom take a critical stance toward the postulate, anachronistic for the early days of Antioch, of a complete separation of the church from association with the synagogue.

[14] Tacitus, *Ann.* XV 44.2; Suetonius, *Nero* 16.2; Pliny, *Ep.* X 96.1-13. It is possible that the separation of Jews and Christians emerged in connection with a conflict, verging on civil war, between the Jewish and Greek populations of Antioch, as Malalas (X 244.15–245.21) reports took place in the third year of Caligula's reign (39–40 C.E.). It is improbable, however, that the Christians were assigned blame for this unrest, as Justin Taylor, "Why Were the Disciples First Called 'Christians' in Antioch? (Acts 11:26)," *RB* 101 (1994) 75–94, assumes as the political-legal background.

[15] This widespread use of the name "Christian" in Antioch or Syria speaks against the thesis of Botermann, *Judenedikt,* 141–88, that the name Χριστιανός was coined between

Even if Barnabas himself did not belong to those men from Cyprus and Cyrene of Acts 11:20 and thus to the founders of the community, he was undoubtedly a leading figure in the early days of Antioch's Christian community and played a substantial role in its development. The organized establishment of a mission to the uncircumcised Gentiles, the start of a genuine Christianity clearly distinguished from Judaism, and the beginnings of autonomy for the Christian community outside the synagogue were all closely tied to the person of Barnabas.

Beginnings of Cooperative Work with Paul

Presumably around 39/40 C.E.—and thus at the high point of the anti-Jewish sentiment in Antioch mentioned by Malalas,[16] which surely affected the city's Christian community as well—Barnabas went to Tarsus. He did this with the intention of persuading Paul, who was staying there following his flight from Jerusalem (Acts 9:30), to join him in his work in Antioch (Acts 11:25-26). This report appears reliable, especially since, according to his own statement, Paul had left Jerusalem by that time and was living in Cilicia (Gal 1:21). The particular choice of Paul as a companion shows that Barnabas was the decisive figure in determining the theological stance of the early Christian community of Antioch and would, through his cooperation with Paul, set its theological tone. That we know essentially nothing about the intellectual formation of the pre-Christian Barnabas and above all possess none of his writings should not necessarily lead us to doubt the quality of his theological education or categorically exclude the possibility he influenced Paul, not least regarding the question of the Law. At the same time one cannot show that the early Paul, certain as his mission to the Gentiles and reassessment of the Torah may have been even in his Damascus experience,[17] possessed the profound understanding of the Law that comes to light in the letters to the Galatians and, above all, to the Romans, and therefore he may have undergone some degree of theological develop-

---

57 and 59 C.E., presumably by Agrippa II, in *Caesarea* (Acts 26:28), and that Acts 11:26 represents a Lukan projection of the name "Christian" back into the early period of Antioch.

[16] Cf. Martin Hengel and Anna Maria Schwemer, *Paul Between Damascus and Antioch: The Unknown Years* (London: S.C.M., 1997). Malalas dates the joint work of Barnabas and Paul as early as ca. 35–36 C.E. (X 242.8-14).

[17] Cf. particularly Christian Dietzfelbinger, *Die Berufung Paulus als Ursprung seiner Theologie* (Neukirchen-Vluyn: Neukirchener Verlag, 1989) 90–147.

ment.[18] There is also little basis for elevating Paul to the position of Barnabas' theological teacher soon after the Paul's arrival in Antioch.[19] An organized mission, presumably directed from the start at the Gentiles, established itself in Antioch entirely independent of Paul: "It is one of the most important established facts that the universal religious community of Antioch, consisting of Jews and Hellenes, developed without Paul (Acts 11:19ff.)."[20] Barnabas was an important participant in this process, and his influence as well as his theological vision enabled him to bring Paul to Antioch. In Paul, Barnabas chose a colleague from whom he could rightfully expect active support for the program of missionary work among the Gentiles of Antioch.[21] Likewise, the call to Antioch offered Paul, who before this time had been forced to fend for himself[22] and had presumably carried out successful missionary activity in Arabia, as well as in Syria and Cilicia (Gal 1:17, 21), the chance to pursue his vocation as missionary to the Gentiles under favorable conditions. For this reason he was willing to surrender his independence and accept temporary subordination to Barnabas as a "junior partner."[23] A further question is how Barnabas became aware of Paul and whether he knew Paul personally prior to their work together in Antioch. The suggestion that Paul and Barnabas may have encountered one another earlier in the Hellenistic synagogue of Jerusalem (Acts 6:9) has

---

[18] Cf. Johannes Weiss, *Das Urchristentum* (Göttingen: Vandenhoeck & Ruprecht, 1914) 1:130: "that he [i.e., Paul] gradually grew into his stature and work out of or in an already existing movement is what one must expect, humanly and historically. In these 14 or 11 years of his effective work until the Council of Jerusalem he was certainly already 'Paul,' but *the* Paul, whom we know from the epistles, would hardly have been fully developed from the beginning."

[19] According to Martin Hengel, *Acts and the History of Earliest Christianity,* trans. John Bowden (Philadelphia: Fortress, 1980), Barnabas' turn to the mission to the Gentiles may have occurred only under Paul's influence; Hengel, "Die Stellung des Apostels Paulus zum Gesetz in den unbekannten Jahren zwischen Damaskus und Antiochien," in James D. G. Dunn, ed., *Paul and the Mosaic Law* (Tübingen: J.C.B. Mohr [Paul Siebeck], 1996), 46: "In my opinion, although Barnabas was the elder, there can be no doubt that, with regard to the question of the law and the overall theological organization of the mission, the learned Paul assumed the leading role."

[20] Wilhelm Bousset, *Kyrios Christos: A History of the Belief in Christ from the Beginnings of Christianity to Irenaeus,* trans. John E. Steely (Nashville: Abingdon, 1970) 120.

[21] Cf. Becker, "Paul and His Churches," 147: "The question might arise, Why did Barnabas bring in Paul rather than someone else? The answer should be clear: Paul was by then known as a theologian who, through his critical attitude towards the law, was very much in line with the development in Antioch."

[22] Joachim Gnilka, *Paulus von Tarsus: Apostel und Zeuge* (Freiburg: Herder, 1996) 56–58.

[23] Nicholas Taylor, *Paul, Antioch, and Jerusalem: A Study in Relationships and Authority in Earliest Christianity* (Sheffield: Sheffield Academic Press, 1992) 143.

a certain plausibility.[24] If Acts 9:26-30 is not a reliable source, then at least the *Christian* Paul may have been known to Barnabas only by reputation before the events of Acts 11:25-26. A significant task of mediation may then have fallen to Peter, whom Paul sought out three years after his conversion and who had ties to the household of Barnabas' relative Mary and her son John Mark (Acts 12:12-17).

The ancient list of offices and names found in Acts 13:1 reflects the structure and hierarchy of the Christian community of Antioch in that, analogous to Mark 3:16-19 and Acts 6:5, it places the most important person first. Significantly, Barnabas appears first, before Simeon Niger, Lucius of Cyrene, and such a renowned person as Manaen, who was raised in Herod's court,[25] while Paul is found at the end. On account of his work in Antioch (Acts 11:26) Paul belonged to the five-member leadership of the community, but clearly in a subordinate position. According to their roles, the Jewish Christian members of the governing body of the Antiochene Christian community, including Barnabas and Paul, were described as prophets and teachers (Acts 13:1). Both functions also appear in the list of offices in 1 Cor 12:28 (cf. Eph 4:11), which may have originated in Antioch.[26]

A reliable assignment of the persons listed in Acts 13:1 to the offices of teacher and prophet is impossible. However, the account of their activities in Acts 11:26 suggests that Barnabas and Paul worked in Antioch more as teachers than as prophets. The office of Christian teacher was characterized primarily by explication of Scripture, instruction to the community, and transmission of the Jesus tradition.[27] Against this background much evidence supports the claim that Paul became familiar with the majority of those traditions of Jesus and preliterary formulas, which he later used in his letters, during his tenure in Antioch at the side of Barnabas.[28]

[24] However, this is considered by Christoph Burchard, *Der dreizehnte Zeuge: Traditions- und kompositionsgeschichtliche Untersuchungen zu Lukas' Darstellung der Frühzeit des Paulus* (Göttingen: Vandenhoeck & Ruprecht, 1970) 160 n. 107, as background for Acts 9:26-30.

[25] According to Acts 13:1 Manaen was a "milk brother" (σύντροφος) of Herod Antipas, meaning he was raised alongside the princes in the court of Herod the Great.

[26] Cf. Helmut Merklein, *Das kirchliche Amt nach dem Epheserbrief* (Munich: Kösel, 1973) 246–48; Alfred F. Zimmermann, *Die urchristlichen Lehrer: Studien zum Tradentenkreis der* διδάσκαλοι *im frühen Urchristentum* (Tübingen: Mohr, 1988) 110–13.

[27] Cf. Heinz Schürmann, "'. . . und Lehrer': Die geistliche Eigenart des Lehrdienstes und sein Verhältnis zu anderen geistlichen Diensten im neutestamentlichen Zeitalter," in Wilhelm Ernst et al., eds., *Dienst der Vermittlung* (Leipzig: St. Benno-Verlag, 1977) 107–47; regarding Acts 13:1 specifically see Zimmermann, *Die urchristlichen Lehrer,* 118–40.

[28] See below.

During the time of their collaboration in Antioch—which may have lasted longer than the one year referred to by Acts 11:26—a worldwide famine occurred during the reign of Claudius, as had been prophesied by Agabus, and this led Barnabas and Paul to travel to Jerusalem to collect donations for relief (Acts 11:27-30). Luke dates this event to the years between 41 C.E. (the beginning of Claudius' reign) and 44 C.E. (death of Agrippa I, Acts 12:20-23). Paul probably did not travel to Jerusalem during that time since, by his own account, he was in the city but once between his conversion and the Apostolic Council, namely for his fifteen-day visit to Cephas (Gal 1:18; cf. Acts 9:26-30). In any case, the existing evidence indicates only localized famines during Claudius' reign (41–54 C.E.), with only one, during the procurate of Tiberius Alexander (46–48 C.E.), affecting Judea (Josephus, *Ant.* XX.51, 101).[29] Perhaps the account of Barnabas and Paul's putative collection of relief funds is based on Luke's postdating a tradition of their journey together to the Apostolic Council and conflating it with the later collections of the Pauline community for Jerusalem.[30] Alternatively, the tradition behind Acts 11:29-30 may have mentioned neither Paul nor the famine under Claudius and concerned a collection that Barnabas began in Antioch during the reign of Agrippa I (41–44 C.E.) and carried alone to Jerusalem. Were this the case, "with this early Antiochene collection, Barnabas would have created at the same time the model for those larger collections that were made obligatory for the entire Gentile Church at the Apostolic Council (Gal 2:10)."[31]

[29] Cf. Emil Schürer, *The History of the Jewish People in the Age of Jesus Christ*, revised and edited by Geza Vermes and Fergus Millar (Edinburgh: T&T Clark, 1973–1987) 1:457.

[30] Cf. the survey of scholarship in Anton Dauer, *Paulus und die christliche Gemeinde im syrischen Antiochia: Kritische Bestandsaufnahme der modernen Forschung mit einigen weiterführenden Überlegungen* (Weinheim: Beltz Athenäum, 1996) 28–35.

[31] Jürgen Roloff, *Die Apostelgeschichte* (Göttingen: Vandenhoeck & Ruprecht, 1981) 183; Hengel, *Acts*. The position of Jürgen Wehnert, *Die Reinheit des "christlichen Gottesvolkes" aus Juden und Heiden: Studien zum historischen und theologischen Hintergrund des sogenannten Aposteldekrets* (Göttingen: Vandenhoeck & Ruprecht, 1997) 264–73, is also worth considering: Acts 11:27-30 was originally concerned with the collection taken up at the Apostolic Council, which Barnabas, after the incident at Antioch, apart from Paul and parallel to the Pauline collections, established for the congregation in Antioch.

The First Missionary Journey

The Departure from Antioch

From Antioch, Barnabas and Paul, who remained subordinate, undertook their so-called first missionary journey (Acts 13–14). As a historical fact this joint mission to Cyprus and Asia Minor is not in doubt. Although he does not refer to it in Galatians 1–2, Paul alludes to it in other places (1 Cor 9:6; 2 Cor 11:25). Independent of the Acts of the Apostles, 2 Tim 3:11 attests to Paul's effectiveness in Antioch (Pisidia), Iconium, and Lystra, despite the troubles plaguing his work. The first missionary journey took place in the early 40s C.E., before the Apostolic Council.[1]

During a gathering for worship the five leading members of the Christian community received instruction from the Holy Spirit to select Barnabas and Paul for missionary service (Acts 13:2). After fasting and praying, the members present formally commissioned these two by the laying on of hands (13:3). If, contrary to the Lukan theory, Barnabas and Paul were considered members of the apostolate of the Twelve in Acts 14:4, 14, the contours of a characteristic *"charismatically-pneumatically founded apostolate* with a clear orientation toward the *mission"*[2] for Antioch, as Acts 13:1-3 implies, become fully recognizable. As apostles, Barnabas and Paul acted on behalf of the Christian community of Antioch and were responsible for its mission.

---

[1] The late dating of the "first missionary journey" to the time between the Apostolic Council and the incident at Antioch (e.g., Günther Bornkamm, *Paul,* trans. D. M. G. Stalker [New York: Harper & Row, 1971] 43–48) fails because it cannot be placed between 48 C.E. (probable date of the Apostolic Council) and 48–49 C.E. (start of the "second missionary journey").

[2] Jürgen Roloff, "Apostel/Apostolat/Apostolizät I. Neues Testament," *TRE* 3 (1978) 430–45, at 435.

Acts 13:5 first reports that Barnabas and Paul were accompanied by John Mark as an assistant (ὑπηρέτης). He appears to have been neither an apostle chosen by the Holy Spirit nor a colleague who enjoyed equal status (συνεργός), but rather to have functioned as a kind of subordinate aide. The double name indicates that John Mark was active in Semitic as well as Greek-speaking Roman regions. He was Barnabas' nephew or cousin (Col 4:10) and, in terms of both history and impact, belongs as much in the orbit of Peter as of Paul. On the one hand he had contact with Peter through the household of his mother Mary (Acts 12:12), is described in the pseudepigraphical 1 Peter as "my son Mark" (1 Pet 5:13), and is said to have written the Gospel of Mark after hearing Peter's preaching.[3] On the other hand, he stands at the side of Paul not only during the mission to Cyprus but also in the letter to Philemon (Phlm 24), and is acknowledged in the Deutero-Pauline corpus (Col 4:10; 2 Tim 4:11).

There is an informative reference in 1 Cor 9:6 to how the joint mission was carried out. Paul's report that he, in agreement with Barnabas, made no claim on the apostles' right to receive financial support from the local community can refer only to their work during the first missionary journey. As a result of this behavior Paul was accused of not being an apostle (1 Cor 9:2), but it provided him with independence from the local leadership and particularly aided missionary activity in urban areas.[4] In all probability Paul was taught by Barnabas in this regard: "As a missionary, Barnabas holds to the same principles as does Paul—and since Barnabas is the elder, he is Paul's teacher: Barnabas and Paul renounce the right of missionaries to be supported by the communities."[5]

The Mission to Cyprus

From Seleucia, a port city in the vicinity of Antioch, the journey took them to Salamis on the eastern coast of Cyprus. The desire to carry out a mission on Cyprus grew out of the interest of Barnabas (Acts 4:36) and other members of the Antiochene Christian community in spreading the

---

[3] Eusebius, *Hist. Eccl.* III 39.15 (Papias); VI 14.5-7 (Clement of Alexandria); VI 25.4-5 (Origen).

[4] Cf. Wilhelm Pratscher, "Der Verzicht des Paulus auf finanziellen Unterhalt durch seine Gemeinden: ein Aspekt seiner Missionsweise," *NTS* 25 (1979) 284–98; Gerd Theissen, "Legitimation und Lebensunterhalt: ein Beitrag zur Soziologie urchristlicher Missionare, in idem, ed., *Studien zur Soziologie des Urchristentums* (Tübingen: J.C.B. Mohr [Paul Siebeck], 1983) 201–30, at 209–14.

[5] Hans Conzelmann, *History of Primitive Christianity*, trans. John E. Steely (Nashville: Abingdon, 1973) 158.

Gospel on their native island. Since parts of Stephen's circle had already reached Cyprus and begun preaching to the Jewish community there (11:19), Barnabas, Paul, and Mark occasionally met Jewish Christians in the island's synagogues. Salamis was the traditional port of debarkation for travelers to Cyprus from the eastern Mediterranean. It had lost the status of capital city to Paphos during the period of Ptolemaic rule, but remained as before the intellectual as well as the economic center of the island and boasted an important temple to Zeus.[6] Acts 13:5 summarizes the work of the missionaries in a single sentence: "And when they arrived in Salamis, they proclaimed the Word of God in the synagogues of the Jews." Given its large Jewish population and later role as the center of the Jewish revolt under Trajan, the city probably contained numerous synagogues. Luke had access to no additional information, and nothing is known of a mission to the Gentiles in Salamis.

From Salamis, Barnabas, Paul, and Mark traveled to Paphos on the western edge of Cyprus, which, as the seat of the Roman proconsul, served as the administrative center of the whole island. More precisely, they went to Nea-Paphos (Pliny, *Nat. Hist.* V.130), which had been founded as a port city with "well-built temples" and stood sixty stadia from Palai-Paphos, a city rich in tradition. Every year a great procession took place from Paphos to the renowned temple of Aphrodite in Palai-Paphos (Strabo, XIV 6.3), which Titus visited in 69 C.E. to consult the oracle during his journey by sea to Syria (Tacitus, *Hist.* II 2.2–4.2). In contrast to Salamis, which was oriented toward the East, Paphos had a strongly Roman character. Around 50 B.C.E. Cicero asked Gaius Sextilius Rufus, as quaestor of Cyprus, to attend to the well-being of the citizens of Paphos with particular care (Cicero, *Fam.* XIII 48). After Paphos was destroyed by an earthquake in 15 B.C.E. Augustus provided financial assistance for rebuilding and bestowed upon the city the title "Augusta/Sebaste" (Dio Cassius, LIV 23.7).

At the time of the Antiochene mission to Cyprus the proconsul in office was Sergius Pau(l)lus (Acts 13:7). Luke does not provide the *praenomen*. Inscriptions refer to two people who may be identified with this Sergius Paul(l)us. The first, which can be only partially reconstructed, is from Chytroi on Cyprus (*SEG* 20:302).[7] It mentions a Quintus

---

[6] Cf. Terence Bruce Mitford, "Roman Cyprus," *ANRW* II 7.2 (1980) 1321–23; idem, "Cults of Roman Cyprus," *ANRW* II 18.3 (1990) 2189ff.

[7] The text is readily available in Greek and German in Cilliers Breytenbach, *Paulus und Barnabas in der Provinz Galatien: Studien zun Apostelgeschichte 13f.; 16:6; 18:23 und den Adressaten des Galaterbriefes* (Leiden: Brill, 1996) 181.

Sergius, who was presumably proconsul on Cyprus during the reign of Gaius Caligula (37–41 C.E.), and who may have been the same Sergius Paul(l)us found in Acts 13:7.[8] Aside from the fact that the *cognomen* Paullus can be only hypothetically assumed for this inscription, assigning such an early date to the first missionary journey is not unproblematic since, at least according to the chronology of the Acts of the Apostles, it took place not during the reign of Caligula but rather during that of his successor, Claudius (Acts 11:28). An inscription from Rome mentions a Lucien Sergius Paullus as one of the trustees responsible for care of the banks of the Tiber during the reign of Claudius (41–54 C.E.) (*ILS* 5926). Since the *nomen gentile* and *cognomen* agree, this may refer to the Sergius Paul(l)us of Acts 13:7, who then would have become proconsul of Cyprus following his service as trustee in Rome.[9]

According to Acts 13:6-8, Sergius Paul(l)us kept company with a Jewish magician named Bar-Jesus Elymas. This Bar-Jesus Elymas acted as a false prophet (Acts 13:6) and may have specialized in divining the future or interpreting dreams or worked as a kind of court astrologer. Pliny spoke of the magic of Cyprus in the same breath as Jewish magic—which, around the beginning of the Common Era, enjoyed the esteem of Gentiles as well[10]—identifying it as an independent movement of magical activity (*Nat. Hist.* XXX 11). Josephus refers to the Cypriot Jew Atomos, who, like Bar-Jesus, served as a magician for the Roman governor, specializing in love spells.[11] The sociocultural shading of the Lukan ac-

---

[8] Justin Taylor, "St. Paul and the Roman Empire: Acts of the Apostles 13–14," *ANRW* II 26.2 (1995) 1194: "It is therefore likely that the proconsul whom Barnabas and Saul met at Paphos was Quintus Sergius Paullus, who is otherwise unknown, and who can be dated to the reign of Caligula, i.e., A.D. 37–41."

[9] Rainer Riesner, *Paul's Early Period: Chronology, Mission Strategy, Theology,* trans. Doug Scott (Grand Rapids: Eerdmans, 1998). Cf. also Breytenbach, *Paulus und Barnabas,* 38–45, 180 (German-Latin text of *ILS* 5926).

[10] Strabo XVI 2.39; Pliny, *Nat. Hist.* XXX 11. Cf. Bernd Kollmann, *Jesus und die Christen als Wundertäter: Studien zu Magie, Medizin und Schamanismus in Antike und Christentum* (Göttingen: Vandenhoeck & Ruprecht, 1996) 118–73.

[11] Josephus, *Ant.* XX 7: "While Felix was procurator of Judea, he saw this Drusilla, and fell in love with her; for she did indeed exceed all other women in beauty; and he sent to her a person whose name was Simon, one of his friends; a Jew he was, and by birth a Cypriot, and one who pretended to be a magician, and endeavored to persuade her to forsake her present husband, and marry him." (*The Works of Flavius Josephus,* trans. William Whiston [Philadelphia: International Press, 1912] 594). See also Josephus, *Ant.* XX 142: "Felix, the governor of Judea, had only just seen Drusilla, who distinguished herself by her great beauty, when he began to burn with ardent love for her. Therefore he sent to her his friend, a Jew by the name of Atomos, who came from Cyprus and passed himself off as a magician, to persuade her to leave her husband and marry him."

count portrays "the ancient context very precisely."[12] It is Paul rather than Barnabas who emerges as the opponent of Bar-Jesus Elymas. The historical kernel of the miracles of Acts 13:9-12 remains obscure. One can certainly imagine that Bar-Jesus Elymas, fearing the loss of his lucrative position, spoke out hostilely against Barnabas and Paul, and when this failed it became the basis for the story of miraculous punishments brought against him.[13] The proconsul Sergius Paul(l)us would hardly have converted to Christianity, but he could have been won as a sympathizer. Presumably the subsequent missionary stations of Barnabas and Paul are connected with Sergius Paul(l)us. As numerous inscriptions indicate, the family of Sergius Paulus had its *patria* in Pisidian Antioch and possessed a considerable amount of land in the province of Galatia. This permits the conjecture "that the proconsul himself advised Paul to continue his journey to Pisidian Antioch, where he could provide introductions to the upper class of the Roman colony."[14]

The events in Paphos had far-reaching consequences for the Lukan portrayals of Paul and, indirectly, Barnabas. Inspired by the similarity to the name of the Roman proconsul, he referred to Saul from then on in the Acts of the Apostles by his Roman *cognomen* Paul (13:9). At the same time, this name change instituted by Luke corresponds to a shift in the relative importance of Paul vis-à-vis Barnabas. Barnabas, who had previously always been named first (Acts 11:30; 13:2, 7), moves to the second position, and, with a few traditional exceptions (Acts 14:12, 14; 15:12, 25), Paul assumes the leadership role, as Acts 13:13, "then Paul and his companions set sail from Paphos," clearly shows. However, this Lukan construct in no way reflects the actual distribution of authority at this point in the first missionary journey.

Barnabas and Paul in Asia Minor

The first stop on the mainland of Asia Minor was Perga. There John Mark took his leave from the others and returned to his native city of

---

[12] Hans-Josef Klauck, *Magic and Paganism in Early Christianity: The World of the Acts of the Apostles,* trans. Brian McNeil (Edinburgh: T&T Clark, 2000).

[13] Cf. Walter Schmithals, *Die Apostelgeschichte des Lukas* (Zurich: Theologischer Verlag, 1982) 123; Stefan Schreiber, *Paulus als Wundertäter: Redaktionsgeschichtliche Untersuchungen zur Apostelgeschichte und den authentischen Paulusbriefen* (Berlin and New York: Walter de Gruyter, 1996) 44.

[14] Stephen Mitchell, "Population and Land in Roman Galatia," *ANRW* II 7,2 (1980) 1053–81, at 1074 n. 134. Cf. also Riesner, *Paul's Early Period;* Breytenbach, *Paulus und Barnabas,* 39–44.

Jerusalem (Acts 13:13). One can only speculate regarding his motives, as Otto Braunsberger's summary illustrates: "The reason for his departure was, according to some, a failure of nerve; to others, too great a dependence on his mother; to others, the diminishing role of his cousin and friend Barnabas as Paul gained authority; to still others, Paul's liberal manner toward the Gentiles, which he found worrisome."[15] This last suggestion, that John Mark no longer wanted to be responsible for the "practice of the mission to the Gentiles without regard to the Law," has enjoyed a certain level of acceptance.[16] However, John Mark may have turned back simply because a mission to Asia Minor had not originally been planned but was added at the suggestion of Sergius Paullus.[17]

Barnabas and Paul made their way to Antioch in Asia Minor, which Acts 13–14, in agreement with Pliny, *Nat. Hist.* V 94, locates in the region of Pisidia, while Strabo places it as "Antioch by Pisidia" in Phrygia (XII 6.4; 8.14). Like Antioch in Syria, it owes its name to the Seleucid king Antiochus the Great (223–187 B.C.E.). At the time of the first missionary journey it was, along with Iconium and Lystra, one of the seven colonies Augustus established in 25 B.C.E. in the south of the Roman province of Galatia in order to pacify the Phrygian-Pisidian border region, and it went by the name *colonia Caesarea Antiochia* (Pliny, *Nat. Hist.* V 94). The great missionary address of Acts 13:16-41, which granted the Jews a final opportunity to convert and definitively proclaimed the transmission of the Gospel to the Gentiles, is a product of Luke and is placed in the mouth of Paul, who, according to the Lukan account, surpassed Barnabas' position after the events in Paphos. The pre-Lukan tradition reliably reports that Paul, as well as Barnabas, preached in the synagogue of Antioch and was able to win over many Jews and proselytes or God-fearers (13:43). Although nothing outside the Acts of the Apostles indicates the existence of a Jewish population or even a synagogue in Antioch itself, we know from Josephus that Antiochus the Great settled two thousand Jewish families in Phrygia and Lydia in order to secure the border (*Ant.* XII 147–153).[18]

---

[15] Otto Braunsberger, *Der Apostel Barnabas: Sein Leben und der ihm beigelegte Brief* (Mainz: Florian Kupferberg, 1876) 55 n. 3.

[16] Jürgen Roloff, *Die Apostelgeschichte* (Göttingen: Vandenhoeck & Ruprecht, 1981) 203ff. The mission to the uncircumcised Gentiles was certainly the fundamental premise of the Antiochene mission (Acts 11:20), under which John Mark got involved with the Cyprus mission and which he later encountered again at Paul's side (Phlm 24), which argues against any fundamental theological differences between the two.

[17] Breytenbach, *Paulus und Barnabas,* 43 n. 79.

[18] Cf. Paul R. Trebilco, *Jewish Communities in Asia Minor* (Cambridge: Cambridge University Press, 1991) 5–7. Evidence from inscriptions from the second century C.E. attests

After being driven out of Antioch, Paul and Barnabas continued along the Via Sebaste, which served as a military highway linking the Roman colonies of southern Galatia,[19] until they reached Iconium (Acts 14:1). This was the fertile and prosperous center of the arid region of Lycaonia, known for its sheep-breeding industry (Strabo XII 6.1; Pliny, *Nat. Hist.* V 95). Administratively the city was divided into two parts: the Roman *colonia Iulia Augusta Iconium* and an independent *polis* made up of non-Roman citizens.[20] All that we know of the Jews there, who reportedly drove the apostles out by stoning them, comes from the account in the Acts of Apostles (Acts 14:4-7).

The subsequent stops on the missionary journey, Lystra and Derbe, are of minimal significance and presumably lacked Jewish populations worthy of mention. Luke does speak generally in Acts 16:3 of "Jews in those places." In reality, however, aside from Timothy's mother who, contrary to Jewish law, had entered into a mixed marriage with a Gentile and had not had her son circumcised (Acts 16:1-3), nothing is known of the Jews living in Lystra and Derbe. There is correspondingly no evidence of the presence of God-fearers in those places. The missionary sermon of Acts 14:14-17 then turned logically to the "genuine" pagans, who were committed to polytheism. In Lystra and Derbe, despite their overall lack of significance, arose the first purely Gentile Christian communities (with the exception of Timothy's mother).

The focal point of the visit to the Roman *colonia Iulia Felix Gemina Lustra,* reported in Acts 14:8-20, is a miracle of healing and its consequences (*CIL* III, 6786). A man lame since birth is healed on account of his faith in Paul with the words, "Stand upright on your feet," and can walk for the first time in his life (14:8-10). Even if elements from Peter's miracle in Acts 3:1-10 are interwoven into this account, it nonetheless began from a kernel of historical truth. Accounts of healing lameness were widespread in antiquity[21]—for instance, at the shrine of Asclepius of Epidauros—and were performed in early Christianity by charismatic miracle workers who

---

to the existence of a Jewish woman named Debbora from a prominent family in Antioch (*MAMA* IV 202), but this does not necessarily refer to Pisidian Antioch. Cf. Justin Taylor, "St. Paul and the Roman Empire," 1207–11.

[19] Cf. D. H. French, "The Roman Road-System of Asia Minor," *ANRW* II 7,2 (1980) 698–729, at 707.

[20] Stephen Mitchell, "Iconium and Ninica, Two Double Communities in Roman Asia Minor," *Historia* 28 (1979) 409–38, at 411–25.

[21] Cf. Ingrid Maisch, *Die Heilung des Gelähmten: Eine exegetisch-traditionsgeschichtliche Untersuchung zu Mk 2:1-12* (Stuttgart: KBW Verlag, 1971) 57–71.

recited such formulas as the one found in Acts 14:10.[22] Paul himself acknowledged that he had performed miracles (Rom 15:19; 2 Cor 12:12).

The detailed acclamation following the miracle (Acts 14:11-13) imparts local color to the narrative. In reaction to the healing of the lame
man, the assembled crowd, speaking in the Lycaonian tongue—which
evidently remained in use in the region around Lystra as late as the
sixth century C.E.—begins paying homage to the apostles as gods in
human form. Barnabas is given the name of Zeus, father of the gods,
while Paul is honored as Hermes, the divine messenger. Inscriptions
provide evidence of the worship of Zeus and Hermes in the area around
Lystra.[23] The acclamation in response to the miracle in Acts 14:11-13 has
as its background the saga, probably of Phrygian origin, of Zeus and
Hermes (Roman Jupiter and Mercury), in which they travel incognito
throughout the world and only receive hospitality from the elderly
couple Philemon and Baucis, who are then richly rewarded while everyone else is punished (cf. Ovid, *Metamorphoses* VIII 620-725). After watch-
ing the healing, the citizens of Lystra obviously wanted to avoid the
mistake of their forebears who had, to their misfortune, failed to recognize Zeus and Hermes. Barnabas originally must have played a much
more central role in the account of the healing than the Lukan narrative indicates.[24] If one assumes that Paul alone performed the miracle,
it is difficult to account for the veneration of Barnabas as a deity. Barnabas clearly not only participated in the healing of the lame man but
was in fact the preeminent figure in the event. The identification of
Barnabas with Zeus and Paul with Hermes, while attributable to Barnabas' greater age, on the one hand, and Paul's perhaps greater elo-
quence, on the other (cf. 2 Cor 10:10; 11:16), also expresses a
hierarchical relationship. Further evidence of this is the phrase, un-
changed by Luke, "the apostles Barnabas and Paul" (Acts 14:14). In the
Lystra tradition Barnabas and Paul, contrary to Luke's exclusive apostolate of the Twelve, are considered apostles (cf. 14:4), and in contrast to
the ranking favored by Luke after Acts 13:13, Barnabas again assumes
the primary position. In combination with his veneration as Zeus this
demonstrates that, as before, Barnabas was the leading figure in the

[22] Cf. Kollmann, *Jesus und die Christen*, 348–55.
[23] Regarding local color in Acts 14:8-20 and the link between 14:12 and the Philemon-
Baucis saga see Justin Taylor, "St. Paul and the Roman Empire," 1216–21, and, above all
Cilliers Breytenbach, "Zeus und der lebendige Gott: Anmerkungen zu Apostelgeschichte
14:11-17," *NTS* 39 (1993) 396–413; idem, *Paulus und Barnabas*, 31–38; 53–75.
[24] Cf. Roloff, *Apostelgeschichte*, 213; Schreiber, *Paulus als Wundertäter*, 70–72.

mission in southern Galatia and the founding of the first purely Gentile Christian congregation—even if Paul did most of the talking.

The subsequent missionary speech (Acts 14:15-17), addressed to the Gentiles, is the work of Luke, though Barnabas and Paul undoubtedly preached Jewish-Christian monotheism to the polytheistic inhabitants of Lystra. If the citizens of Lystra began worshiping the living God of the Bible, creator of all things, in place of Zeus, whom they venerated as a nature deity, they would face not only religious consequences. In response to the healing miracle the priest of the temple of Zeus had made opulent preparations for the sacrifice of a bull before the city gates of Lystra (14:13). Usually such sacrifices offered only part of the animal, often the inedible innards, to the deity, while the rest was set aside for consumption. Acts 14:13, "he wanted to offer sacrifice with the crowd," concerns a public meal, which would have provided the better part of the citizenry of Lystra with a rare opportunity to eat meat.[25] The Lystran people's anger resulted in the first place from the fact that they felt cheated out of a lavish meal by the monotheistic preaching of Barnabas and Paul (14:18), and they vented their frustration with a stoning (14:19), a widespread form of vigilante justice common in the ancient world (Apuleius, *Metamorphoses* X 6.3). Contrary to Luke's assertions, Jews from Antioch and Iconium can scarcely have been involved.[26] This is very likely the same stoning Paul refers to in 2 Cor 11:25 without specifying the time or place.

Luke reports that, following their departure from Derbe after the successful establishment of a congregation there, the missionaries Paul and Barnabas traveled via Lystra, Iconium, Antioch, and Perga to the port city of Attalia to begin the return journey by sea to Syrian Antioch, where they presented an account of their activities to the assembled community (Acts 14:20b-27). Historically speaking it is questionable whether Barnabas and Paul returned in such a short space of time to all those places they had visited prior to the stoning. More likely they may have journeyed home by way of the shorter though more difficult land route over the Taurus Mountains through the Cilician gap. Luke had

---

[25] Regarding the Hellenistic sacrificial meal cf. Hans-Josef Klauck, *Herrenmahl und hellenistischer Kult: Eine religionsgeschichtliche Untersuchung zum ersten Korintherbrief* (Münster: Aschendorff, 1982) 45–49.

[26] Klauck, *Magic and Paganism,* regarding Acts 14:19: "Luke often proceeds in such a way that he goes beyond the reports of his sources and introduces Jewish opponents as the primary fomenters of unrest (cf., e.g., 2 Cor 11:32 with Acts 9:23-25). That is without question a highly problematic aspect of his work, which we ought not accept uncritically."

access to no precise information from the period, presumably of several years, between the return to Antioch and the departure for the Apostolic Council, and confined himself to the statement that Barnabas and Paul stayed "for some time" with the disciples at Antioch (14:28). During this time they probably continued teaching in the Christian community (11:26) and may also have pursued joint missionary work in the Syrian regions around Antioch.

The Apostolic Council
and the Break with Paul

The So-called Apostolic Council

Following the first missionary journey we see Barnabas playing a leading role in the epochal[1] event of early Christian history usually called the Apostolic Council, recounted in Gal 2:1-10 and Acts 15:1-33. This was a gathering in Jerusalem at which a delegation from the Christian community of Antioch, led by Barnabas and Paul, and important members of the Jerusalem community, namely the three pillars James, Cephas, and John, took part. A third faction, present in the background, was made up of Jewish Christians from Jerusalem who favored strict adherence to the Law and were not included in the eventual settlement. Paul characterizes them as "false brothers" (Gal 2:4), and they were most likely, as Acts 15:5 asserts, former Pharisees. It can be deduced from the statements of Gal 2:1 that the gathering took place fourteen years after Paul's first visit to Jerusalem as a Christian and thus approximately seventeen years after his Damascus experience, likely in the year 48 C.E. The Apostolic Council sought to address a problem that had arisen from the Antiochene Christian community's idea of a mission directed at the Gentiles and came to a head with the founding of the first clearly Gentile Christian congregations in Lystra and Derbe:[2] Is it

[1] Cf. Jürgen Roloff, *Neues Testament* (Neukirchen-Vluyn: Neukirchener Verlag, 1977) 47: "In it [i.e., the Apostolic Council] all the strands of the preceding nearly twenty-year-long history of early Christianity come together and, at the same time, it set the decisive course for the further progress of events."

[2] However, the European mission was not a forerunner of the Apostolic Council but rather is part of the subsequent history since, instead of the early dating of the founding of the Corinthian congregation to 41 C.E. (Gerd Lüdemann, *Paul, Apostle to the Gentiles: Studies in Chronology,* trans. F. Stanley Jones [Philadelphia: Fortress, 1984]; Joachim Gnilka, *Paulus von Tarsus: Apostel und Zeuge* [Freiburg: Herder, 1996] 64–71), 49 C.E. remains the most probable date (cf. Rainer Riesner, *Paul's Early Period: Chronology, Mission Strategy, Theology,* trans. Doug Scott [Grand Rapids: Eerdmans, 1998]; Helga Botermann, *Das Judenedikt*

legitimate to convert Gentiles to Christianity without obligating them to obey the Torah in its entirety, above all its requirement of circumcision for males? At the Apostolic Council this question was answered in the affirmative, and the necessity of full observance of the Law for salvation was denied.

It is also evident from Gal 2:4 and Acts 15:1, 24 that a circle of strict Jewish Christians from the community of Jerusalem argued for an undiminished obligation of Torah obedience for Gentile Christians. In this regard the demand for male circumcision (Gal 2:3; Acts 15:1) was a key point. Whether these Pharisaically-educated Jewish Christians came to Antioch, as Acts 15:1 asserts, or were only active in Jerusalem, stirring up public opinion against the mission to the uncircumcised Gentiles, as Gal 2:4 claims, is an open question. In any case an Antiochene delegation, under the leadership of Paul and Barnabas, made its way to Jerusalem to work out a solution to the problem. The delegation also included Titus (Gal 2:3), a Gentile Christian, perhaps a native of Antioch, who had been converted by Paul (cf. Titus 1:4) and who became the symbolic figure of the agreement reached in Jerusalem. He was the test case that was to prove the legitimacy of the Antiochene missionary practice. That Titus, whose circumcision was vehemently demanded by the so-called false brothers, left the Apostolic Council still uncircumcised served, in Paul's view, as living proof that the Antiochene missionary concept was accepted in principle by the Jerusalem authorities.

At the conclusion of the Apostolic Council a division of responsibilities was established and the agreement sealed by an offering of the right hand of fellowship. Paul and Barnabas were legitimized as missionaries to the uncircumcised Gentiles, while the original congregation, with Peter clearly serving as an especially active missionary, would still proclaim among the Jews a message of continued adherence to the whole of the Torah (Gal 2:7-9). The duty to take up a collection for the Christian community of Jerusalem, connected with the account of the Apostolic Council (Gal 2:10),[3] ought to be viewed against the historical backdrop of the famine that afflicted Judea between 46 and 48 c.e. (Josephus, *Ant.* XX 51, 101). Barnabas was included in this agreement to take up a collection, as Gal 2:10 ("They asked only one thing, that *we* remember the poor, which was actually what

---

des Kaisers Claudius: Römischer Staat und Christiani im 1. Jahrhundert [Stuttgart: Steiner, 1996] 29–49), and consequently the second missionary journey should be placed after the Apostolic Council, in agreement with the Acts of the Apostles.

[3] Cf. Dieter Georgi, *Der Armen zu gedenken: Die Geschichte der Kollekte des Paulus für Jerusalem* (Neukirchen-Vluyn: Neukirchener Verlag, 1994) 13–30.

I was eager to do") shows beyond doubt. How Barnabas carried out this duty after his break with Paul remains unknown, provided Acts 11:27-30 does not distort the facts. Extensive support, as Paul strongly emphasized (Gal 2:6, 10), was not forthcoming. Contrary to the Lukan account (Acts 15:19-29), the so-called apostolic decree was not a document of the agreement reached at the Apostolic Council but rather belonged in the context of the incident at Antioch described in Gal 2:11-14.

The portrayal of events in Gal 2:1-10 is focused entirely on the person of Paul and reflects his disagreement with his opponents, who favored rigorous obedience to the Law and who had infiltrated the congregations of Galatia. The role of Barnabas in the Jerusalem negotiations is inevitably forced into the background. It is true, however, that Paul was the leader of the Antiochene delegation at the Apostolic Council and that his initiative was behind the use of the uncircumcised Titus as a demonstration. As before, with regard to their views of the Law, Barnabas and Paul stood in complete agreement, though Paul emerged from Barnabas' shadow to become the primary champion of freedom from ritual law. From this point on it is he who shapes the Antiochene theological position vis-à-vis the mission to the uncircumcised Gentiles and consistently represents this position to the larger community. Conversely, it ought to be emphasized that Barnabas, as Paul's equal partner, won the acceptance of the Antiochene missionary principle[4] and, unlike the case of Titus, that principle is included *expressis verbis* in the agreement reached with the three pillars, James, Cephas, and John (Gal 2:9). At the time of the Apostolic Council, Barnabas unquestionably belonged among the five most important figures in early Christianity, who determined the fate of the Church.

The Incident at Antioch

Soon after the Apostolic Council, the so-called incident at Antioch took place,[5] not only leading to heightened tensions between Peter and

---

[4] Martin Hengel and Anna Maria Schwemer, *Paul Between Damascus and Antioch: The Unknown Years* (London: S.C.M., 1997) 209 ("At that time Barnabas was a conversation-partner with equal rights . . . . Barnabas, who was familiar with conditions in Jerusalem and was esteemed there, will have played at least an equal part in the success.") It ought to be taken into account here that the Jerusalem agreement, which Barnabas had also advocated, may have signaled approval in non-Pauline missionary regions also to follow the Antiochene position regarding circumcision. Cf. Jürgen Becker, *Paul, Apostle to the Gentiles,* trans. O. C. Dean, Jr. (Louisville: Westminster John Knox, 1993) 93–99.

[5] It is unlikely that the Antiochene crisis was the cause of the Apostolic Council and accordingly preceded the latter (Lüdemann, *Paul* [101–105]). Even if he employs the stylistic

Paul but also foreshadowing the break between Paul and Barnabas. We know of this event only from Gal 2:11-14. In evaluating the conflict in general and the role of Barnabas in particular it ought to be recalled that Paul, when he recounted the incident at Antioch, was in the midst of an emotional debate with opponents in Galatia, and this situation strongly colors his account.

Galatians 2:11-14 makes clear that, after the Apostolic Council, Paul and Barnabas returned to Antioch, and a short time later Cephas arrived there as well. Since the community of Antioch had a relatively large share of Gentile Christians, who did not feel bound to follow Jewish ritual laws, Jewish ritual standards were not observed during the meals shared by Jewish and Gentile Christians. Galatians 2:11-14 leaves the details unclear. In particular certain Jewish purification rites, such as washing before eating (Mark 7:3) and purifying eating utensils (Mark 7:4), were not performed. Additionally, impure meat—in extreme cases even meat that had been sacrificed to idols—may have appeared on the tables.[6] While observant Jews would not even have considered such table fellowship with Gentiles,[7] the Jewish Christians of Antioch, most notably Paul and Barnabas, had no reservations about eating with Gentiles since they had adopted a new view of the Torah. Cephas, too—who according to Acts 11:3 had already shared a table with the Gentile centurion Cornelius—freely conformed to the liberal practice of Antioch after his arrival there (Gal 2:12).

The entire situation changed abruptly upon the arrival in Antioch of a group of people sent by James from Jerusalem. Clearly word of the ac-

---

technique of the *narratio,* Paul proceeds chronologically in Galatians 1–2 (Hans Dieter Betz, *Galatians* [Philadelphia: Fortress, 1979] 104; Traugott Holtz, "Der antiochenische Zwischenfall (Galater 2:11-14)," *NTS* 32 (1986) 344–61), and Acts 15:36-40 likewise dates the break with Barnabas to the period after the Apostolic Council.

[6] Regarding Jewish dietary laws in New Testament times see Christoph Heil, *Die Ablehnung der Speisegebote durch Paulus: Zur Frage nach der Stellung des Apostels zum Gesetz* (Weinheim: Beltz Athenäum, 1994) 23–123. Nicholas Taylor, *Paul, Antioch and Jerusalem: A Study in Relationships and Authority in Earliest Christianity* (Sheffield: Sheffield Academic Press, 1992) 126, points out the economic aspect of the dietary practices of the Antiochene Christian congregation, noting "that food bought in the Jewish markets in Antioch would have been more expensive than food not subject to the specific requirements of the Law" (cf. Josephus, *Bell.* II 591-94).

[7] Cf. 3 Macc 3:4 ("they [i.e., the Jews] feared God and lived according to his law, they kept their separateness with regard to foods and for this reason appeared hateful to some"); *Jubilees* 22:16 ("Separate from the nations, and do not eat with them. . . . Do not become their companion, for their actions are something that is impure . . ."); from the pagan perspective Diod. Sic. XXXIV 1.2; XL 3.4; Strabo XVI 2.37; Tacitus, *Hist.* V 5.2.

tions of Cephas, who had been assigned the mission to the Torah-observant Jews at the Apostolic Council (Gal 2:7), had reached Jerusalem, so James felt compelled to return Cephas to the position of the Jewish Christians who remained true to the Law. The Christian community of Jerusalem, which had been under intense Jewish pressure from the time of persecution under Herod that had culminated in the martyrdom of James the son of Zebedee (Acts 12:1-17), must have considered it a significant threat when one of its most prominent representatives so grievously violated the Torah's laws of purity, as was the case with Peter in Antioch. At the time of the Apostolic Council, at which he appeared as head of the three-member group governing the community (Gal 2:9), James the Lord's brother had become the leading figure in the Christian community and, as Gal 2:11-14 illustrates, claimed an authority far beyond the bounds of Jerusalem.[8] There is, however, no basis for the suggestion that James fundamentally revised his view of the mission to the Gentiles in light of the Apostolic Council. Since the people sent by James to Antioch demanded neither male circumcision nor observance of the entire Torah, this did not represent a "betrayal" of the settlement reached in Jerusalem, especially given the fact that Paul nowhere raises any charges of breaking the agreement. The concern here is with an aspect of the Law question not considered at the Apostolic Council and in need of clarification in light of the common practice in Antioch that had become known in Jerusalem, namely, the matter of observance of Jewish dietary laws in the context of communal meals of Gentile and Jewish Christians. What James' people wanted to accomplish in Antioch was a return of the city's Jewish Christians to observance of the Torah's laws of purity. With regard to the Gentile Christians, they had presumably already propagated the demands of the "apostolic decree," generally considered a result of the incident at Antioch (Acts 15:19-21; 21:25).[9]

In these "James clauses" Gentile Christians who associate with Jewish Christians are required to observe a minimum of cultic purity. Referring back to the regulations of Lev 17:8-16 and 18:6-18, they obligate

---

[8] Cf. Martin Hengel, "Jakobus der Herrenbruder—der erste 'Papst'?" in Erich Gräber and Otto Merk, eds., *Glaube und Eschatologie* (Tübingen: J.C.B. Mohr [Paul Siebeck], 1985) 88 ("claims of authority that concerned not only the Jewish Christian congregations"); more cautious is Wilhelm Pratscher, *Der Herrenbruder Jakobus und die Jakobustradition* (Göttingen: Vandenhoeck & Ruprecht, 1987) 78–80.

[9] Cf. Becker, *Paul, Apostle to the Gentiles,* 97–98, and, better, Jürgen Wehnert, *Die Reinheit des "christlichen Gottesvolkes" aus Juden und Heiden: Studien zum historischen und theologischen Hintergrund des sogenannten Aposteldekrets* (Göttingen: Vandenhoeck & Ruprecht, 1997) 129–43, 267–70.

Gentile Christians to abstain from those foods and sexual relations that had been forbidden to foreigners living in Israel. The dietary regulations forbid the consumption of meat that has been offered to idols, blood, and whatever has been strangled. This last refers to animals that have not been slaughtered according to Jewish law (cf. Lev 17:15) and therefore symbolically have been suffocated by their own blood.

Cephas changed his behavior immediately after the arrival of the people sent by James and kept himself separate from the Gentile Christians (Gal 2:12). This amounted to a *de facto* termination of the shared Lord's Supper meal, since the communal meals in Antioch included the Supper within the setting of a regular meal.[10] Cephas' aim was not the division of the community into Jewish Christian and Gentile Christian factions with permanently separate dining arrangements, but rather the development of new guidelines for communal meals. Cephas had successfully compelled the Gentile Christians to follow the Jewish way of life (ἰουδαίζειν) (Gal 2:14), in that he made the restoration of shared meals dependent on the acceptance of certain Jewish dietary laws, presumably the "James clauses" of the so-called apostolic decree. Paul labeled this behavior fickle hypocrisy, inspired by a scaredy-cat attitude toward the people sent by James (φοβούμενος τοὺς ἐκ περιτομῆς). The vehemence of Paul's reaction is understandable only when viewed against the backdrop of the earlier Apostolic Council. Paul would hardly have opposed a respect for Jewish dietary regulations if it resulted from the commandment to love, as shown by his later appeal for consideration of those weak in faith, who clearly continued to observe the Jewish ritual laws (Rom 14:1-21).[11] However, in the demand of people sent by James that Gentile Christians observe the Jewish dietary laws Paul sees an attempt to sneak through the back door a renewed understanding of the Law as the means of salvation and to torpedo the mission to the uncircumcised Gentiles that had been granted to Barnabas and him at the Apostolic Council. In the final analysis, in Paul's view this matter concerned the most important question of all: whether salvation depended upon Christ as its only foundation or whether the return to an understanding of the Law as an authority relevant to salvation was imminent.

Since for Paul the path to salvation "free of the law" was at stake in the incident at Antioch, it must have been particularly painful for him

[10] Cf. Holtz, "Der antiochenische Zwischenfall," 348–51.
[11] These weak ones were most likely Jewish Christians who, out of fear of cultic impurity, abstained from certain foods (Rom 14:2) and also continued observing Jewish holidays as they had before (14:5). Cf. Heil, *Speisegebote,* 243–65.

that, along with Cephas, Barnabas adopted the position of the people sent by James. Correspondingly, he too was accused of hypocrisy. Nevertheless, can one really conclude from Gal 2:13 that Barnabas was only oriented toward the Antiochene Gentile Christians as long as Peter took his side and that he then followed his exemplar Peter back to the synagogue?[12] For Barnabas himself, his position represented a concession to observant Jewish Christians, born of a willingness to compromise, and in no way affected his fundamental attitude toward the mission to the Gentiles. In this case Barnabas was true to his reputation as a "bridge-builder"[13] and proved to be a man of reconciliation who, within the framework of the mission to the uncircumcised Gentiles, sought to preserve the unity of Jewish and Gentile Christians within the Church by offering concessions. Presumably he was also aware of the negative consequences of his attitude toward the people sent by James, which could result in a general rejection of the Torah's laws of purity by Jewish Christians in the troubled community of Jerusalem. This does not change the fact that at first Barnabas, in agreement with Paul's position, took part in the Antiochene communal meals, which were not obligated to conform to the purity standards of the Torah, and he had now taken a step in the opposite direction, which Paul, in light of the fundamental significance of the matter, must have seen as a hypocritical desertion to the opposing camp.

Given the position of renown that Barnabas held in the Christian community of Antioch (Acts 13:1), his actions had a signal effect on the other Jewish Christians and, most importantly, led to a shift in influence to the detriment of Paul. All the evidence indicates that Paul came up short in the incident at Antioch and, in the end, stood in nearly complete isolation.[14] The catchphrase characterizing Antioch as "Paul's

[12] Becker, *Paul, Apostle to the Gentiles,* 96, takes this position. Lothar Wehr, *Petrus und Paulus—Kontrahenten und Partner: Die beiden Apostel im Spiegel des Neuen Testaments, der Apostolischen Väter und früher Zeugnisse ihrer Verehrung* (Munster: Aschendorff, 1996) 68–71, rightly emphasizes that Peter changed his conduct primarily out of concern for the unity of the church and acted in no way out of fear or opportunism. For an overview of research see Andreas Wechsler, *Geschichtsbild und Apostelstreit: Eine forschungsgeschichtliche und exegetische Studie über den antiochenischen Zwischenfall (Gal 2:11-14)* (Berlin and New York: Walter de Gruyter, 1991) 1–295.

[13] According to the apt characterization found in H. Evans, "Barnabas the Bridge-Builder," *ExpT* 89 (1977/78) 248–50.

[14] Cf. Walter Radl, "Das 'Apostelkonzil' und seine Nachgeschichte, dargestellt am Weg des Barnabas," *ThQ* 162 (1982) 45–61, at 59–60. Silas seems simply to have moved into alignment with him and been chosen as his new coworker (Acts 15:40).

trauma"[15] is not without justification. He saw no grounds for continued work with Barnabas and broke off contact with him, as well as with the entire Christian community of Antioch. No longer dependent on Antioch and estranged from Barnabas, he began to labor again as a solitary missionary.

According to the Acts of the Apostles as well, a bitter fight took place, with Paul and Barnabas consequently going their separate ways (Acts 15:36-40). In that account, however, the falling out is attributed to Barnabas' insistence on the participation of John Mark in further missionary undertakings, to which the Lukan Paul objected because he deemed John Mark unreliable on account of his earlier desertion during the first missionary journey (Acts 13:13; 15:38). Arguing against these basic reservations about John Mark is Philemon 24, in which he appears again as one of Paul's fellow workers. Either Luke was unaware of the bitter theological controversy over observance of the Jewish dietary laws that led to the split, or else he sought to provide an innocuous explanation for the break between Paul and Barnabas, attributing it to a personal rather than a theological dispute.

The Continuing Work of Barnabas

Barnabas' actions during the incident at Antioch did no harm to his reputation, as indirectly indicated by the widespread acceptance in early Christianity of the demands of the "apostolic decree."[16] Despite their arguments, Paul remained in agreement with Barnabas regarding the central principles of missionary work and used this in debates with his opponents. If Barnabas' refusal to accept financial support from the local community is cited in 1 Cor 9:6 as a guarantee of the legitimacy of the Pauline apostolate, he must have been considered an apostle even by the Christians of Corinth, who were entirely unacquainted with him, and been a renowned figure in the church. There was not, however, a renewal of his work with Paul. The statement of the *Acts of Peter* that Barnabas, along with Timothy, worked beside Paul in Rome before Paul

[15] Anton Dauer, *Paulus und die christliche Gemeinde im syrischen Antiochia: Kritische Bestandsaufnahme der modernen Forschung mit einigen weitererführenden Überlegungen* (Weinheim: Beltz Athanäum, 1996) 127.

[16] Holtz, "Der antiochenische Zwischenfall," 355: "The regulations of the decree immediately took effect in the whole church. . . . One could say that not only in Antioch but also in the entire early church James, Peter, and Barnabas had won. And one could add: not without reason." Regarding the general acceptance of the "apostolic decree" see Wehnert, *Reinheit des "christlichen Gottesvolkes,"* 145–208.

set off on his mission to Spain[17] deserves no confidence. The same holds true for the tradition, retold in many forms since the Middle Ages, of Barnabas' mission to northern Italy, which served the purely apologetic end of providing the church of Milan with an apostolic foundation.[18]

After his split from Paul, Barnabas, who by this time clearly must have been more than fifty years old, resumed his missionary activities, as 1 Cor 9:6 suggests. After the incident at Antioch he set off, together with John Mark, on a new mission to Cyprus (Acts 15:39), at which point he disappears from the Acts of the Apostles and reliable information about him comes to an end. The gaps are filled in with legends from such sources as the pseudepigraphic *Acts of Barnabas by John Mark* and the *Laudatio* of Alexander Monachus, whose respective accounts of the second Cyprus mission and the death of Barnabas concur in outline. Accompanied by John Mark, Barnabas carried out missionary work over the whole of Cyprus and suffered martyrdom in Salamis at the hands of local Jews stirred up by Bar-Jesus Elymas (*ActBarn* 23) or Jews who had traveled there from Syria (Alex. Mon., *Laudatio* 26.479–29.549) before his corpse was finally buried, along with a copy of the Gospel of Matthew, by John Mark. Around the year 488 c.e., during the reign of Emperor Zeno (474–491), the alleged gravesite of Barnabas was discovered northwest of Salamis in a cave under a carob tree.[19]

The legendary accounts may correspond to historical fact insofar as they claim that Barnabas died during the second Cyprus mission, whether by violence or of natural causes. At least a rough timeframe can be determined for the date of his death. At the time that 1 Corinthians was written Barnabas was still alive, or at least Paul had received no word of his death (1 Cor 9:6).[20] According to Alexander Monachus, John

---

[17] *Act Petr* 4: "And the brethren were exceedingly disturbed, especially as Paul was not at Rome, nor Timothy and Barnabas, whom Paul had sent to Macedonia." John K. Elliot, *The Apocryphal New Testament: A Collection of Apocryphal Christian Literature in an English Translation* (Oxford: Clarendon Press, 1993) 401.

[18] Cf. Richard A. Lipsius, *Die apokryphen Apostelgeschichten und Apostellegenden: Ein Beitrag zur altchristlichen Literaturgeschichte* (Braunschweig: Schwetschke und Sohn, 1884) 2/2:305–20. Opposing this is Otto Braunsberger, *Der Apostel Barnabas: Sein Leben und der ihm beigelegte Brief* (Mainz: Florian Kupferberg, 1876) 112, according to whom "the preaching of the apostle Barnabas in northern Italy" should be considered "not entirely certain but nonetheless very probable."

[19] Theodorus Lector, *Historia Ecclesiastica* (ed. G. Ch. Hansen), Epitome 436; Alex. Mon., *Laudatio* 41.758-72; Suda s.v. θύϊνα (Adler II.733).

[20] Cf. Braunsberger, *Barnabas*, 79: "From our passage [i.e., 1 Cor 9:6] it emerges that at the time of the writing of the First Letter to the Corinthians the death of Barnabas either had not yet occurred or had occurred so recently that Paul was not yet aware of it."

Mark brought news of Barnabas' death to Paul in Ephesus (*Laudatio* 30.553-55). When considered alongside 1 Cor 9:6, this suggests that Barnabas died around 55 C.E. June 11 was chosen as the official day of remembrance for Barnabas' death.

Barnabas as Representative of the Antiochene Theology

One of the lasting contributions of the "history of religions school" has been its drawing attention to the existence of a pre-Pauline Hellenistic Christianity, to which Paul owed essential elements of his theological thought as well as his knowledge of various traditional materials.[21] The two locations where such a handing on of tradition must have taken place are Damascus and Antioch. Although the theological influence of the Hellenistic Jewish Christian community of Damascus on Paul should not be underestimated (Acts 9:10-25), Antioch indisputably played a key role in the development of the pre-Pauline tradition. Assuming Paul arrived in Antioch around 39/40 C.E., the church there could already look back on a history of close to seven years. During these years, in the course of an organized mission to the Gentiles, a Christian community developed that encompassed both Jews and Greeks and whose theological currents influenced Paul before he gradually began his active ministry. If one is looking for a theological head in the early years of the Antiochene Christian community, one who decisively shaped its development, hardly anyone besides the teacher (Acts 11:26) and community leader (Acts 13:1) Joseph Barnabas even deserves consideration. "If one wanted to name the Antiochene theology of the mission to the Gentiles after a particular individual, it would not be called Pauline theology but rather the theology of Barnabas."[22]

In terms of sources that shed light on the pre-Pauline Antiochene theology—whose contours, despite all the imponderables involved, emerge quite clearly—we must refer extensively to the letters of Paul.

---

[21] Cf. Wilhelm Heitmüller, "Zum Problem Paulus und Jesus," *ZNW* 13 (1912) 320–37, at 330 ("Paul is separated from Jesus not only by the early Christian community but also by another intervening element. The series of developments proceeds: Jesus—early community—Hellenistic Christianity—Paul"); Wilhelm Bousset, *Kyrios Christos: A History of the Belief in Christ from the Beginnings of Christianity to Irenaeus*, trans. John E. Steely (Nashville: Abingdon, 1970) 119–22; Rudolf Bultmann, *Theology of the New Testament*. 2 vols., trans. Kendrick Grobel (New York: Charles Scribner's Sons, 1951) 1:63–64.

[22] Andreas Feldtkeller, *Identitätssuche des syrischen Urchristentums: Mission, Inkulturation und Pluralität im ältesten Heidenchristentum* (Freiburg: Universitätsverlag; Göttingen: Vandenhoeck & Ruprecht, 1993) 136.

Of utmost importance is the fact that the majority of the pre-literary formulas that are implicitly or explicitly recognizable as pre-existing traditions Paul adopted from the community are likely of Antiochene origin.[23] In this regard 1 Thessalonians, written not long after the incident at Antioch, deserves special attention insofar as it, as a document dating from the early period of Paul's independent missionary work and still showing a strong Antiochene influence, differs in character from later Pauline letters.[24]

When Paul refers expressly to the directions for the Lord's Supper given in 1 Cor 11:23b-25 and the christological formula of 1 Cor 15:3b-5 as earlier traditions he had received, he is speaking of traditions he first became familiar with during his work in Antioch at Barnabas' side.[25] First Corinthians 11:23b-25 represents the "Antiochene model" of the Lord's Supper, also favored by Luke (Luke 22:15-20), in which the double action of the sacrament takes place in the context of a full meal and reflects, in the words accompanying the cup, the community's consciousness of itself as the heir of the new covenant, promised in Jer 31:31-34 and established by the blood of Christ. With the addition of the anamnesis a new interpretation appears that, influenced by Hellenistic meals in honor of the dead, places in the foreground the historical origins of the Lord's Supper in the context of Jesus' crucifixion.[26] Barnabas and Paul introduced this form of the Lord's Supper in the congregations they founded during

---

[23] Cf. especially Ludger Schenke, *Die Urgemeinde: Geschichtliche und theologische Entwicklung* (Stuttgart: Kohlhammer, 1990), 326–47; Walter Schmithals, *The Theology of the First Christians,* trans. O. C. Dean, Jr. (Louisville: Westminster John Knox, 1997) 81–84; 99–113; Eduard Lohse, *Paulus: Eine Biographie* (Munich: Beck, 1996) 80; regarding pre-literary forms Philipp Vielhauer, *Geschichte der urchristlichen Literatur: Einleitung in das Neue Testament, die Apokryphen und die Apostolischen Väter* (Berlin and New York: Walter de Gruyter, 1975) 9–57. Taking a hypercritical stance toward pre-Pauline Antiochene theology are Hengel and Schwemer, *Paul Between Damascus and Antioch,* 286–310.

[24] Jürgen Becker, "Paul and His Churches," in idem, ed., *Christian Beginnings: Word and Community from Jesus to Post-Apostolic Times,* trans. Annemarie S. Kidder and Reinhard Krauss (Louisville: Westminster John Knox, 1993) 146; idem, *Paul, Apostle to the Gentiles,* 102–12, 130–40; Feldtkeller, *Identitätssuche,* 135–38. The lack of a doctrine of justification in 1 Thessalonians may be the result of the particular situation and hardly justifies the assumption that Barnabas and Paul had not yet reflected on the problematic of the Law during the course of their mission to the Gentiles (see above).

[25] Cf. Günther Bornkamm, "Herrenmahl und Kirche bei Paulus," in idem, *Studien zur Antike und Urchristentum: Gesammelte Aufsätze* (3rd ed. Munich: Kaiser, 1970) 2:138–76, at 147; Schenke, *Urgemeinde,* 112–14, 338.

[26] Cf. Hans-Josef Klauck, *Herrenmahl und hellenistischer Kult: Eine religionsgeschichtliche Untersuchung zum ersten Korintherbrief* (Munster: Aschendorff, 1982) 314–17; Bernd Kollmann, *Ursprung und Gestalten der frühchristlichen Mahlfeier* (Göttingen: Vandenhoeck & Ruprecht, 1990) 184–87.

their first missionary journey. It was also presumably the model for those communal meals in Antioch that Peter, under pressure from the people sent by James, stopped attending (Gal 2:11-14). Both 1 Cor 11:23b-25 and 1 Cor 15:3b-5 are constitutively shaped by an interpretation of Jesus' death as vicarious suffering "for us" or "for our sins," a theological position Paul was already familiar with when he wrote 1 Thessalonians (1 Thess 5:10). The Hellenistic Jewish Christian community of Antioch is clearly the place where as a result of taking up the christological tradition of an expiatory sacrifice, as in Rom 3:24-26, a deepened soteriological interpretation of Jesus' death as vicarious suffering for sins emerged.[27]

In our considerations of the beginnings of the Christian community in Antioch[28] it became clear that the systematic rejection of male circumcision was legitimated with formulas like those found in 1 Cor 7:19, Gal 5:6, and Gal 6:15 and thus that a presumably pre-Pauline understanding of baptism, which was seen to abolish the differences between Jews and Greeks in Christ (1 Cor 12:13; Gal 3:26-28), stands in the background. Key ideas from the shared Antiochene missionary work of Barnabas and Paul can be uncovered in 1 Thess 1:9b-10 and 1 Cor 8:6. The former refers back to Paul's founding sermon in Thessalonica, which took place in 49 C.E. Since it occurred soon after the break with Antioch its content reflects Antiochene customs. During his European mission, as before, Paul used the practices developed during his missionary preaching to the Gentiles in Antioch. He first demands a renunciation of polytheism and a turn to the living God of the Bible—as Acts 14:15-17; 17:23-27, and Heb 6:1 all illustrate independently of 1 Thess 1:9b-10[29]—and follows this with proclamations about christology and eschatology. Eschatological topics addressed in 1 Thess 1:10 include the *parousia* of Jesus and his saving role in the Last Judgment, but not the resurrection of the dead. The unqualified prominence of the expectation of the *parousia* clearly represents another characteristic of early Antiochene theology, which Paul gradually abandoned as his eschatology developed (1 Cor 15:20-58; 2 Cor 5:1-10).[30] Likewise directed

---

[27] Schenke, *Urgemeinde,* 338 ("The death of Jesus was interpreted for the first time in terms of substitutionary atonement"); Becker, "Paul and His Churches," 151 ("It was apparently the Greek-speaking Jewish Christians in Syria who for the first time interpreted Jesus' death as an expiatory suffering on our behalf [1 Cor 15:3b-4; 1 Thess 5:10]").

[28] See above.

[29] Cf. Ulrich Wilckens, *Die Missionsreden der Apostelgeschichte: Form- und traditionsgeschichtliche Untersuchung* (Neukirchen-Vluyn: Neukirchener Verlag, 1974) 81–91, 190–93.

[30] Udo Schnelle, *Wandlungen im paulinischen Denken* (Stuttgart: Katholisches Bibelwerk, 1989) 37–48.

strongly against heathen polytheism and in that regard closely related to the missionary kerygma of 1 Thess 1:9b-10 is the pre-Pauline acclamation of 1 Cor 8:6. The εἷς θεός formula, adopted from the proselytizing of Diaspora Judaism, is set aside in favor of the christological expression εἷς κύριος, and this is expanded by reference to the theology of the mediating role of the preexisting *Kyrios Iesous Christous* in the creation of all things. Paul encountered this tradition in the course of his Antiochene work as well, since Antioch was the place where both the theology of the preexistent Christ and the recognition of Jesus Christ as the *Kyrios* took on their definitive form.[31] This suggests an Antiochene origin for other passages as well, for example the hymn of Phil 2:6-11, which presents the preexistent and exalted Jesus Christ as *Kyrios* over the whole cosmos.

The extent of Barnabas' contribution to development of these ideas in early Antiochene theology cannot be more precisely determined. Limits are established by the fact that the pre-Pauline traditions were shaped, to a degree that should not be underestimated, by the theological thinking of Stephen's circle, to which Barnabas was certainly connected in Jerusalem.[32] Beyond this one should also consider that because of Paul's later involvement in the theological development of Antioch it is difficult to find a clear break between the traditions of the Antiochene community and the early Pauline tradition, and consequently in certain contexts "pre-Pauline" may overlap with "early Pauline."[33] Undoubtedly christology developed in Antioch in particular in a manner that proved to be of fundamental importance for Paul's theology, as well as for the history of early Christian theology in general. One would not be out of line in seeing Barnabas as the leading theological light of the pre-Pauline Christian community of Antioch. Not only was he from the start or at least very early a champion of the mission

---

[31] Cf. Becker, "Paul and His Churches," 144–55; regarding in particular the Antiochene coining of *Kyrios* as a christological title of sovereignty see Bousset, *Kyrios Christos*, 149–50; Schenke, *Urgemeinde*, 342–47; Eckhard Rau, *Von Jesus zu Paulus: Entwicklung und Rezeption der antiochenischen Theologie im Urchristentum* (Stuttgart: Kohlhammer, 1994), 83–86. However, Schmithals, *Theology of the First Christians*, 94–102, seeks to make Damascus a plausible cradle for the christology of preexistence and, with reference to Rom 1:3-4, to reclaim for Antioch an "adoption christology."

[32] This relates not only to the soteriological interpretation of Jesus' death but also, for instance, to the christology of preexistence, for which Stephen's circle, reverting to the idea of preexisting Wisdom, may have provided the "initial spark." Cf. Helmut Merklein, "Zur Entstehung der urchristlichen Aussage vom präexistenten Sohn Gottes," in idem, ed., *Studien zu Jesus und Paulus* (Tübingen: J.C.B. Mohr [Paul Siebeck], 1987) 247–76.

[33] Becker, *Paul, Apostle to the Gentiles,* 104.

to the uncircumcised Gentiles, but, as a teacher, he must also have participated substantially in the creation of the christological tradition of Antiochene pre-Pauline Hellenistic Jewish Christianity. The early Antiochene theology, discernible in the letters of Paul, reflects in its fundamentals not least the theological thought of Barnabas.

Later Traditions
About Barnabas

Barnabas' significance and fame are also attested indirectly by the history of works both by and about him. Barnabas was said to be the author of two important letters and a gospel. In addition to numerous scattered traditions from the early church, three comprehensive biographies, namely the pseudepigraphic *Acts of Barnabas by John Mark,* the *Laudatio Barnabae* of Alexander Monachus, and the *Acta Bartholomaei et Barnabae* are dedicated to accounts of his life.

The Letter to the Hebrews

When Tertullian, after his turn to Montanism, attacked the church's penitential customs—far too liberal, in his eyes—in *De Pudicitia* ("On Respectability"), he tried to support the righteousness of his own rigorism with evidence from the New Testament writings. In this regard he referred to a "Writing of Barnabas to the Hebrews," which enjoyed great respect in the churches, and cited from it Heb 6:4-8 (*Pud.* 20). Tertullian thus used Barnabas as the representative of an early Christian rigorism that objected to the renewed repentance of baptized Christians.

On the basis of this tradition, transmitted by Tertullian, of a highly regarded document written by Barnabas for the Hebrews, Barnabas was often thought to have been the true author of the New Testament letter to the Hebrews.[1] The simultaneous closeness to and distance from Pauline theology that characterizes the letter to the Hebrews and its Hellenistic Jewish Christian features both support such an attribution.[2]

---

[1] Cf. Hans-Friedrich Weiss, *Der Brief an die Hebräer* (Göttingen: Vandenhoeck & Ruprecht, 1991) 63.

[2] Cf. Friedrich Blass, *(Barnabas) Brief an die Hebräer* (Halle: Niemeyer, 1903) 9; John A. T. Robinson, *Redating the New Testament* (London: S.C.M., 1976) 215–20.

Conversely, the radical rejection of the Old Testament cultic laws in Heb 10:1-18 represents no insurmountable barrier to Barnabas' possible authorship[3] if he associated with the Hellenists surrounding Stephen in the Jerusalem community and was, both in Antioch and at the Council of Jerusalem, a crucial supporter of the mission to the Gentiles. On the whole the grounds for attributing the letter to the Hebrews to Barnabas are certainly not nearly sufficient, and "who wrote the epistle is known to God alone."[4] It is thus impossible to use the letter to the Hebrews as a primary source for Barnabas' theological ideas, however appealing such a possibility might be.

The Letter of Barnabas

From the time of its initial mention by Clement of Alexandria, the *Letter of Barnabas* was attributed to Paul's companion of the same name.[5] However, he could not have been the author because the *Letter of Barnabas* is, in all probability, the product of a Gentile Christian. No former Jew could have characterized the conversion to Christianity in the first person plural as a renunciation of idol worship and described his pre-Christian past with the words "before we believed in God" (*Barn.* 16:7). In addition, the *Letter of Barnabas* occasionally betrays unfamiliarity with Jewish rituals (7:4; 8:1), and Paul's associate Barnabas was no longer alive in the second century c.e., when this work presumably was written.[6]

The particular significance of this pseudepigraphic letter for the history of Barnabas' influence is its claim to make Joseph Barnabas an au-

---

[3] For an opposing view see Werner Georg Kümmel, *Introduction to the New Testament,* trans. Howard Clark Kee (Nashville: Abingdon, 1975) 402: "But could Barnabas, a Levite from Cyprus (Acts 4:36) who later took up residence in Jerusalem and was a highly respected member of the community there (Acts 9:27; 11:22) have so completely abandoned the position of the primitive community with regard to the law and cultus? Could he have become so rhetorically trained and so Hellenistically oriented as to become the author of Heb?"

[4] Origen, according to Eusebius, *Hist. Eccl.* VI 25.14.

[5] Clement of Alexandria, *Strom.* II 116.3; V 63.1. Regarding the numerous references of Clement of Alexandria to the *Letter of Barnabas* see Adolf von Harnack, *Geschichte der altchristlichen Literatur bis Eusebius,* Vol. I: *Die Überlieferung und der Bestand* (Leipzig: J. C. Hinrichs, 1893) 58–62.

[6] Probable date of composition is the period between 130 and 140 c.e. since *Barn.* 16:3-4 clearly refers to the placing of a shrine to Jupiter on the Temple Mount in Jerusalem, ordered by Hadrian in 130 c.e. Cf. Philipp Vielhauer, *Geschichte der urchristlichen Literatur: Einleitung in das Neue Testament, die Apokryphen und die Apostolischen Väter* (Berlin and New York: Walter de Gruyter, 1975) 610–12; Klaus Wengst, *Didache (Apostellehre), Barnabasbrief, Zweiter Klemensbrief, Schrift an Diognet* (Darmstadt: Wissenschaftliche Buchgesellschaft, 1984) 114–18.

thoritative voice supporting Christian freedom from Jewish ceremonial law. Especially important against the backdrop of the incident at Antioch is the interpretation of the Old Testament dietary laws in *Barn.* 10:1-12. The fundamental axiom here is that when Moses spoke of the prohibition against eating unclean animals he meant this in a spiritual sense, while the Jews believed incorrectly that he referred to the actual rejection of certain foods (10:9). The true intent of the laws in question, for the author of the *Letter of Barnabas,* was to command avoidance of contact with people characterized by various qualities suggesting resemblance to animals deemed unclean by the Mosaic Torah.[7] Old Testament laws regarding sacrifice (*Barn.* 2:1-10), circumcision (9:4-6), and Sabbath observance (15:1-9) are likewise given spiritual interpretations. Whoever pseudepigraphically attributed to the historical Barnabas such an attitude toward the Torah cannot have assigned any importance to Barnabas' actions during the incident at Antioch and must have placed Barnabas firmly on the side of those early Christians, represented by Paul, who favored freedom from the Jewish ceremonial laws.

Barnabas in Pseudo-Clement

In Pseudo-Clement, Barnabas appears as a close confidante of Peter and plays a central role in the conversion of Clement. Barnabas was already included in the version of Clement's work[8] underlying both the *Recognitions* and the *Homilies,* although their respective portrayals of Barnabas differ.

According to the *Recognitions of Pseudo-Clement* (I 7.1-11.8), Barnabas went to Rome during Jesus' lifetime, where he spread the news of Jesus' teachings and miracles. With his monotheistic missionary preaching, which demanded a turn to the *one* God who governed both heaven and earth (I 7.4-6),[9] Barnabas succeeded in converting Clement, purported to

[7] Regarding allegorical interpretation of ritual law in the *Letter of Barnabas* cf. James Carleton Paget, *The Epistle of Barnabas: Outlook and Background* (Tübingen: J.C.B.Mohr [Paul Siebeck], 1994) 143–54, 211–14; Reidar Hvalvik, *The Struggle for Scripture and Covenant: The Purpose of the Epistle of Barnabas and Jewish-Christian Competition in the Second Century* (Tübingen: J.C.B. Mohr [Paul Siebeck], 1996), 119–28.

[8] Regarding the common model of the *Recognitions* and the *Homilies* cf. Georg Strecker, *Das Judenchristentum in den Pseudoklementinen* (Berlin: Akademie Verlag, 1981) 35–96, 255–67; Johannes Irmscher, introduction to "The Pseudo-Clementines," in Wilhelm Schneemelcher, *New Testament Apocrypha,* Vol. II: *Writings Related to the Apostles, Apocalypses, and Related Subjects,* trans. R. McL. Wilson (Philadelphia: Westminster, 1965) 532–35.

[9] Cf. Eduard Norden, *Agnostos Theos: Untersuchungen zur Formengeschichte religiöser Rede* (Darmstadt: Wissenschaftliche Buchgesellschaft, 1956) 3–12.

be a relative of Emperor Tiberius, to the Christian faith. Clement offered Barnabas protection from an angry mob and later followed him to Judea, where Barnabas had traveled to celebrate an unnamed Jewish holiday (I 10.4). In Caesarea Clement was taken by Barnabas to Peter (I 12.1-13.4). In contrast, the *Homilies of Pseudo-Clement* report that not Barnabas but an unidentified missionary arrived in Rome (*Hom.* I 7.1-8), and his preaching inspired Clement to journey to Judea. On account of a storm he went first to Alexandria, where he met Barnabas (I 9.1; II 4.1), who later introduced him to Peter in Caesarea (I 15.1-9).

On the whole the portrayal of Barnabas in the *Recognitions* takes priority on this point,[10] especially since the *Acts of Peter* also reports a visit by Barnabas to Rome—though later, in the time of Nero (*Act Petr* 4). Those passages of Pseudo-Clement that mention Barnabas are particularly significant because they provide evidence of Barnabas' amicable relationship with Peter and praise Barnabas as the one most deeply penetrated with divine wisdom (*Recogn.* I 12.6). Pseudo-Clement, with its anti-Pauline orientation, does not refer to the relationship of Barnabas and Paul.

The Acts of Barnabas

The *Acts of Barnabas*, whose exact title reads Περίοδοι καὶ μαρτύριον τοῦ ἁγίου Βαρνάβα τοῦ ἀποστόλου, claims to be the work of John Mark. In reality it was written long after his death, and because of its precise geographical detail the author had to have been a Cypriot extraordinarily familiar with his native island. A probable date for its writing is the end of the fifth century C.E., as it appears to assume the discovery of the apostle's gravesite under Emperor Zeno (474–491 C.E.). In contrast to other apocryphal acts of various apostles, which seek to edify and entertain, the *Acts of Barnabas* pursues a concrete ecclesio-political goal, namely to prove the independence of the church of Cyprus. In the historical background stands the assertion, going back to the Council of Ephesus (431 C.E.) and made again with renewed emphasis by the Antiochene patriarch Petrus Fullo around 488 C.E., that the church of Cyprus was subject to the authority of the bishop of Antioch.[11] At the heart of this conflict was the

---

[10] Cf. Richard A. Lipsius, *Die apokryphen Apostelgeschichten und Apostellegenden: Ein Beitrag zur altchristlichen Literaturgeschichte* (Braunschweig: C. A. Schwetschke und Sohn, 1883–844) II/2:271ff.; Norden, *Agnostos Theos*, 4 n. 2; Birger A. Pearson, "Earliest Christianity in Egypt: Some Observations," in idem and James E. Goehring, eds., *The Roots of Egyptian Christianity* (Philadelphia: Fortress, 1986) 132–59 at 136–37.

[11] Cf. Karl Baus and Eugen Ewig, *Die Reichskirche nach Konstantin dem Großen*, Vol. I: *Die Kirche von Nikaia bis Chalkedon* (Freiburg: Herder, 1973) 248.

question of the apostolicity of the church of Cyprus, which tried to sub-
stantiate its claim to autonomy by seeking evidence of its apostolic origins and the existence of an apostle's grave in its territory. Accordingly,
the overall purpose of the *Acts of Barnabas* is "none other than to portray
Barnabas as the apostle of Cyprus and attribute to him the establishment
of the church there and the consecration of the first bishop, but above all
to claim his grave for Cyprus."[12]

Fully a third of the *Acts of Barnabas* (1–10) runs parallel to the account
in the Acts of the Apostles, recounting, with some changes and embell-
ishments, first the joint mission of Barnabas, Paul, and John Mark, and
then the incident at Antioch and Barnabas' split from Paul. The most
extensive section by far of the *Acts of Barnabas* (11–26) is dedicated to
the gaps left after Acts 15:39 and covers the period from the second mission to Cyprus to the martyrdom of Barnabas. In Laodicea, south of Antioch, Barnabas and John Mark board a boat bound for Cyprus, but a
storm drives them far off course to mainland Asia Minor. From there
they set off for Krommyakites in northern Cyprus and then travel
through Lapithos, Lampadistos, and Tamassos to Paphos on the island's
southwestern coast. Finally they journey east along the southern coast
through Kurion, Amathus, and Kition to Salamis, where Barnabas suffers martyrdom. Bar-Jesus Elymas plays a central role in the account,
frequently stirring up the island's Jews against Barnabas (*Act Barn*
18–20), which finally leads to Barnabas' violent death in Salamis (*Act
Barn* 23).

The *Acts of Barnabas* offers a valuable source of information about
Cyprus's topography and its Hellenistic cults. Aside from its aforementioned ecclesio-political goal of proving the apostolicity of Cyprus, the
text is of little significance for the history of theology. Of special note,
however, are the baptism narrative of *Act Barn* 12–13, which uses the
garment symbolism of Gal 3:27, and the work's indications of a close association of Barnabas with the Gospel of Matthew (*Act Barn* 15, 22, 24).

The *Laudatio Barnabae* of Alexander Monachus

Much more clearly than the *Acts of Barnabas,* the *Laudatio Barnabae* of
Alexander Monachus, written in the sixth century c.e., proves to be "a
propaganda piece produced to support the ecclesiastical independence

---

[12] Lipsius, *Die apokryphen Apostelgeschichten,* 290. Regarding the history of the church in
Cyprus see also Bonnie B. Thurston, "Christian Cyprus I: Beginnings through the Old
Catholic Period (from Barnabas to Constantine)," to be published in *ANRW* II 24.

of Cyprus."[13] Alexander lived as a monk in the monastery that had been established beside the church at Barnabas' gravesite northwest of Salamis. Long stretches of the work are dedicated to the controversy discussed above between the church of Cyprus and the bishop of Antioch and its favorable outcome. Following the discovery of the apostle's grave, the copy of Matthew's gospel found with Barnabas was given as a gift to Emperor Zeno, who in return recognized the autonomy of the church of Cyprus (*Laudatio* 31.570–50.897).

For our purposes the important parts of the *Laudatio* are those dedicated to the *vita* of Barnabas (*Laudatio* 9.145–29.549), for which Alexander Monachus found source material in the *Stromata* of Clement of Alexandria and "other ancient texts" (*Laudatio* 8.136-39). Of particular interest is the way Alexander satisfies, with legendary accounts, the curiosity raised by Acts 4:36 about Barnabas' life before his sale of the field (*Laudatio* 10.161–15.271). Barnabas leaves Cyprus for Jerusalem as a child and becomes a student of Gamaliel, then a follower of Jesus. He converts his aunt Mary, accompanies Jesus to Galilee, is chosen as the first of the Seventy, and, in response to Jesus' preaching (Luke 12:33), gives up all his possessions except for a single field, which he likewise surrenders after Jesus' death. All Barnabas' attempts to convert Paul, the persecutor of Christians, whom he knew from their time together as students of Gamaliel, are in vain (16.271-76).

In its conclusion the account largely follows the narrative of the Acts of the Apostles, in which Barnabas takes Paul to the apostles after his Damascus experience, then goes to Antioch and, with Paul, whom he has brought there, sets off on the first missionary journey and eventually participates in the Council of Jerusalem (*Laudatio* 17.291–23.437). However, the *Laudatio* includes, before the missionary work with Paul in Antioch—between Acts 11:24 and 11:25, as it were—a visit by Barnabas to Rome and Alexandria (*Laudatio* 20.365–21.386) and, like the *Recognitions of Pseudo-Clement*, portrays Barnabas as the first preacher of the Gospel in Rome and founder of the city's Christian congregation. Inspired by Acts 15:36-40, Alexander, like the *Acts of Barnabas* but without reliance upon it, then recounts the break with Paul, the second mission to Cyprus, and the martyrdom in Salamis (*Laudatio* 24.438–29.549).

[13] Lipsius, *Die apokryphen Apostelgeschichten,* 298. The authoritative edition is Peter van Deun, "Sancti Barnabae laudatio auctore Alexandro Monacho," in *Hagiographica Cypria,* 80–122.

The *Acta Bartholomaei et Barnabae*

The *Acta Bartholomaei et Barnabae* (Περίοδοι καὶ μαρτύριον τῶν ἁγίων ἀποστόλων Βαρθολομαίου καὶ Βαρνάβα), presumed to date from the eleventh century C.E. and available since 1993 in a new edition by Peter van Deun,[14] "are not acts of the apostle in the usual sense but rather two encomia cobbled together artificially."[15] The relevant section about Barnabas (51–226) tells the whole life story of the apostle from his birth to his martyrdom in Cyprus and ends by reporting that, during the time of Emperor Zeno, Barnabas appeared to the Cypriot bishop Anthemios and told him the location of his grave. This is an excerpt from the *Laudatio Barnabae* of Alexander Monachus, on which the *Acta Bartholomaei et Barnabae* relies.[16]

The Gospel of Barnabas

Both the *Decretum Gelasianum* (sixth century C.E.) and the "Index of the Sixty Canonical Books" (seventh century C.E.) refer to an apocryphal work called the *Gospel of Barnabas*, whose content remains a mystery. There are, however, two apocryphal sayings of Barnabas that come from neither the letter to the Hebrews nor the *Letter of Barnabas* and that may have been part of this *Gospel of Barnabas*, known today by name only,[17] or from the section of Alexander Monachus' *Laudatio Barnabae* concerned with the appearance of Jesus.

Since the early eighteenth century two extant versions of the *Gospel of Barnabas*, one Spanish and one Italian, have attracted increasing interest from scholars.[18] The Italian version, which encompasses 222 chapters and is kept at the Austrian National Library in Vienna, has

---

[14] Peter van Deun, *"Sanctorum Bartholomaei et Barnabae vita pro menologio imperiali conscripta,"* in *Hagiographica Cypria,* 124–35.

[15] Schneemelcher, *New Testament Apocrypha,* 2:578.

[16] Cf. van Deun in *Hagiographica Cypria,* 63–71, especially 68–71.

[17] One of these sayings is found in the *Codex Bodleianus Baroccianus,* 39 (Greek text in Harnack, *Geschichte der altchristlichen Literatur* 1:62) and reads, "The apostle Barnabas said, 'In difficult contests the victor is the more wretched, for he emerges as the one who has committed the greater sin.'" The second apocryphal saying of Barnabas, "consuming as easily as twigs the despisers of the Godhead," is cited as "Holy Scripture" by Gregory of Nazianzus, *Orationes* XLIII 32.

[18] Regarding the discovery and reception of the *Gospel of Barnabas* see Christine Schirrmacher, *Mit den Waffen des Gegners: Christlich-muslimische Kontroversen im 19. und 20. Jahrhundert dargestellt am Beispiel der Auseinandersetzung um Karl Gottlieb Pfanders "Mîzân al-haqq" and Rahmatullâh ibn Halîl al Utmânî al-Kairânawîs "Izhâr al-haqq" und der Diskussion über das Barnabas-evangelium* (Berlin: K. Schwartz, 1992) 247–356.

been available since 1907 in a complete edition with an English translation.[19] The Spanish version of the *Gospel of Barnabas,* once believed to have vanished entirely sometime in the late eighteenth century, has been available in an incomplete form since the unexpected discovery of a manuscript in 1976 and is now housed at the Fisher Library at the University of Sydney.[20]

This *Gospel of Barnabas* is a late medieval work, presumably dating from between the fourteenth and sixteenth centuries, which brings together Christian and Muslim elements. The source was perhaps the Franciscan Fra Marino, who discovered the *Gospel of Barnabas* in the private library of Pope Sixtus V (1585–1590) and then promptly converted to Islam, as the prologue of the Spanish version attests.[21] Thus it is within the realm of possibility, if unprovable, that this late pseudepigraphic work was based on the ancient *Gospel of Barnabas* or at least incorporates some parts of it. In accordance with the New Testament gospel tradition, the life of Jesus from the Annunciation to the Ascension is recounted. Barnabas, one of the twelve apostles (*Ev Barn* 14), receives the instruction to write the gospel directly from Jesus (*Ev Barn* 221). Christologically, the *Gospel of Barnabas* strongly emphasizes the human nature of Jesus and strictly denies that Jesus is the Son of God or Messiah. While Jesus is assumed directly into heaven after the Last Supper, Judas suffers crucifixion in his stead (*Ev Barn* 217).

Not least because Jesus repeatedly acknowledges Muhammad as the prophet who will succeed him and as the savior of the world, the *Gospel of Barnabas* enjoys high regard in Muslim circles today.[22] For those seeking knowledge of the historical Barnabas, however, it is entirely without merit. Of interest to us nevertheless is the Spanish prologue's assertion—unverifiable in the works of Irenaeus known to us—that Fra Marino became aware of the existence of a *Gospel of Barnabas* from a work of Irenaeus, in which he appealed to Barnabas for support of his position. If this was in fact the case, then a gospel claiming Barnabas' authorship was known as early as the second century C.E.

[19] Lonsdale Ragg and Laura Ragg, *The Gospel of Barnabas Edited and Translated from the Italian Manuscript in the Imperial Library at Vienna* (Oxford: Clarendon Press, 1907). German translation by S. M. Linges, *Barnabasevangelium.*

[20] Cf. John E. Fletcher, "The Spanish Gospel of Barnabas," *NovT* 18 (1976) 314–20 (including a preliminary edition of the prologue).

[21] Regarding the question of authorship cf. the relevant considerations in David Sox, *The Gospel of Barnabas* (London: Allen & Unwin, 1984) 49–73.

[22] Cf. Sox, *Gospel of Barnabas,* 9–32, 77–137; Schirrmacher, *Waffen des Gegners,* 286–385.

Conclusion

When Gregory of Nazianzus, in his encomium of Basil the Great, cites the apocryphal saying of Barnabas, "Despisers of the Godhead are consumed as easily as twigs," to describe Basil's uncompromising attitude toward his opponents (*Orationes* XLIII 32), he closes with the words, "Even though Barnabas stood by Paul during conflicts, he was indebted to Paul for choosing him and making him his partner." Contrary to the actual circumstances of their joint work (Acts 11:25-30), Barnabas is here demoted to the role of an associate chosen by Paul. He moves into the overarching shadow of the Apostle to the Gentiles and is never again able to free himself. Our investigation of Joseph Barnabas has led to the opposite conclusion. In terms of both history and impact, he proves to be a central figure of early Christianity whose significance for the early history of Christian theology and the formation of the church has long been overlooked.

Barnabas, as a Cypriot Levite, was one of those Greek-speaking Jews who, like Paul, were born and raised in the Diaspora, and who maintained close contact with the Palestinian motherland through family connections and on account of their command of Hebrew and Aramaic. At a point not precisely known, though at a relatively advanced age, Barnabas moved to Jerusalem. There, presumably in the context of the Pentecost event, he came in contact with followers of Jesus and, after experiencing a vision of Christ, joined the Christian community, in which he soon played an important role. With his sale of a field, the germ of the "early Christian communal system," Barnabas introduced ideas of the renunciation of possessions and a solidarity based on equality, neither of which was in any way self-evident. This impulse toward social action is also reflected in the later collection of donations for the Christian community at Jerusalem (Acts 11:27-30), which may have served as the model for the collections taken up by Paul.

As a Diaspora Jew with close ties to the motherland, Barnabas was pre-destined to be a mediator, negotiating the boundary between Hebrews and Hellenists, and he enjoyed the respect of both factions of the Christian community. Theologically he stood closer to Stephen and his followers than to the Twelve. This explains why, upon his move to Antioch, Barnabas immediately became a leader in the local Christian community (Acts 13:1), preparing the way for the mission to the Gentiles, and par-ticipated significantly in the Christian church's gradual shift toward understanding itself as an entity separate from the synagogue. Even though much remains unknown in this regard, Barnabas must, in his years as a Christian teacher, have had a decisive effect on the development of the Antiochene theological tradition. At the same time—in what would prove to be his most important contribution—he became the sponsor of Paul, to whom, as his colleague in Antioch, he offered the opportunity to pursue his calling as apostle to the Gentiles within an established organi-zation, and whose theological development he influenced to a degree that should not be underestimated. For the better part of their joint mission to Cyprus and Asia Minor it was Barnabas, rather than his "junior partner" Paul, who set the tone and shaped the missionary style (1 Cor 9:6), until Paul gradually emerged from Barnabas' shadow and became the leading advocate of the Antiochene mission to the Gentiles.

This development does not alter the fact that at the Council of Jeru-salem Barnabas supported Paul's cause, helping to bring about the de-cisive shift toward recognition of the legitimacy of preaching the Gospel without requiring adherence to the Jewish ritual laws, and at that time was among the five most important persons in the church. His actions during the incident at Antioch do not represent a return to strict obser-vance of the Torah but rather express a willingness to compromise, characterized by consideration of the Christian community of Jerusa-lem, which continued to follow Jewish Law. Here again Barnabas proves to be a person who seeks reconciliation. To stay true to his Gospel mes-sage, Paul had to insist on the complete freedom of the Christian from the ritual laws, since otherwise a return to the Law as the source of sal-vation could result. Barnabas did not want to take such a radical step and risk permanently severing ties with the observant Jews. Perhaps the tragedy of Barnabas is that at that time he wanted to maintain something that simply could not last, namely, the unity of the church made up of Jews and Gentiles. Contrary to Barnabas' hopes, Paul's suc-cessful defense of his position during the incident at Antioch became the decisive step toward a Gentile Christian, universal church.

His actions during the incident at Antioch did no damage to Barnabas' reputation during or after his lifetime. Even after they went their separate ways, Paul made use of Barnabas' authority (1 Cor 9:6). As the purported author of the letter to the Hebrews and the *Letter of Barnabas,* Barnabas continued to be claimed as a partisan of the Gospel message of "freedom from the Law." At the same time he enjoyed high repute among the Jewish Christians, represented by Pseudo-Clement, who strongly opposed Paul, and the legends of Cyprus, which guarded his reputation, later told of his special connection to the Gospel of Matthew. The course of these later traditions, at first glance bizarre, was shaped not by coincidence but rather by history. Like Peter, Barnabas was considered a mediator between the two poles of early Christianity, which held opposing views of the Law, and thus he was particularly well suited to be an integrating figure. Not only during his lifetime but also long after his death Barnabas proved to be a "bridge-builder" of inestimable significance, and it is an irony of history that a gospel falsely attributed to him has further widened the cleft between Christianity and Islam.

The obscure existence Barnabas has eked out in New Testament scholarship is entirely unjustified. His enduring significance consists in the fact that he, like no other, appears in a leading role in all the prominent events of early Christianity. As a member of the Christian communities of Jerusalem and Antioch, as a participant in both the Council of Jerusalem and the incident at Antioch, he substantially influenced the fate of Christianity in the first century C.E. Joseph Barnabas, the Levite from Cyprus, deserves a status equal to that of Peter, James, and Paul as a founding figure of the Christian church.

Chronology[1]

Late first century B.C.E.	Birth of Barnabas on Cyprus
?	Barnabas' move to Jerusalem
30 C.E.	Crucifixion of Jesus
After 30 C.E.	Barnabas joins the Christian community of Jerusalem. Sale of a field and donation of proceeds to the community.
32 C.E.	Suppression of Stephen's followers. Calling of Paul.
32/33 C.E. (?)	Founding of the congregation of Antioch by dispersed followers of Stephen. Barnabas' move to Antioch.
Between 37 and 41 (39/40?) C.E.	Start of Paul and Barnabas' cooperative work in Antioch.
Between 41 and 44 C.E.	Barnabas' collection for the Jerusalem Christian community (Acts 11:29)
After 43/44 C.E. (?)	Barnabas' mission with Paul to Cyprus and Asia Minor
48 C.E.	Apostolic Council
48/49 C.E.	Incident at Antioch. Barnabas' break with Paul and start of a new mission to Cyprus with John Mark.
c. 55 C.E.	Death of Barnabas on Cyprus
c. 488 C.E.	Discovery of Barnabas' alleged grave near Salamis.

[1] For comparisons to the "traditional" Pauline chronology followed here see Jürgen Becker, *Paul, Apostle to the Gentiles,* trans. O. C. Dean, Jr. (Louisville: Westminster John Knox, 1993) 17–32; Rainer Riesner, *Paul's Early Period: Chronology, Mission Strategy, Theology,* trans. Doug Scott (Grand Rapids: Eerdmans, 1998); Udo Schnelle, *The History and Theology of the New Testament Writings,* trans. M. Eugene Boring (London: S.C.M., 1998) 15–28.

Bibliography

Baur, Ferdinand Christian. *The Church History of the First Three Centuries.* Trans. Allan Menzies. London: Williams and Norgate, 1978.

Becker, Jürgen. "Paul and His Churches," in Jürgen Becker et al., eds., *Christian Beginnings: Word and Community from Jesus to Post-Apostolic Times.* Trans. Annemarie S. Kidder and Reinhard Krauss. Louisville: Westminster John Knox, 1993, 132–210.

———. *Paul, Apostle to the Gentiles.* Trans. O. C. Dean, Jr. Louisville: Westminster John Knox, 1993.

Berger, Klaus. *Theologiegeschichte des Urchristentums: Theologie des Neuen Testaments.* Tübingen: Francke, 1995.

Billerbeck, Paul, and Hermann Leberecht Strack. *Kommentar zum Neuen Testament aus Talmud und Midrasch.* 4 vols. Munich: Beck, 1922–1928.

Bornkamm, Günther. *Paul, Paulus.* Trans. D. M. G. Stalker. New York: Harper & Row, 1971.

Botermann, Helga. *Das Judenedikt des Kaisers Claudius: Römischer Staat und Christiani im 1. Jahrhundert.* Stuttgart: F. Steiner, 1996.

Bousset, Wilhelm. *Kyrios Christos: A History of the Belief in Christ from the Beginnings of Christianity to Irenaeus.* Trans. John E. Steely. Nashville: Abingdon, 1970.

Braunsberger, Otto. *Der Apostel Barnabas: Sein Leben und der ihm beigelegte Brief.* Mainz: Florian Kupferberg, 1876.

Breytenbach, Cilliers. *Paulus und Barnabas in der Provinz Galatien: Studien zu Apostelgeschichte 13f.; 16:6; 18:23 und den Adressaten des Galaterbriefes.* Leiden: Brill, 1996.

Burchard, Christoph. *Der dreizehnte Zeuge: Traditons- und kompositionsgeschichtliche Untersuchungen zu Lukas' Darstellung der Frühzeit des Paulus.* Göttingen: Vandenhoeck & Ruprecht, 1970.

Conzelmann, Hans. *Acts of the Apostles: A Commentary on the Acts of the Apostles.* Trans. James Limburg, A. Thomas Kraabel, and Donald H. Juel, ed. Eldon Jay Epp and Christopher R. Matthews. Philadelphia: Fortress, 1987.

———. *History of Primitive Christianity.* Trans. John E. Steely. Nashville: Abingdon, 1973.

Dauer, Anton. *Paulus und die christliche Gemeinde im syrischen Antiochia: Kritische Bestandsaufnahme der modernen Forschung mit einigen weiterführenden Überlegungen.* Weinheim: Beltz Athenäum, 1996.

Feldtkeller, Andreas. *Identitätssuche des syrischen Urchristentums: Mission, Inkulturation und Pluralität im ältesten Heidenchristentum.* Göttingen: Vandenhoeck & Ruprecht; Zürich: Universitätsverlag, 1993.

Gnilka, Joachim. *Paulus von Tarsus: Apostel und Zeuge.* Freiburg: Herder, 1996.

Haenchen, Ernst. *The Acts of the Apostles: A Commentary.* Trans. Bernard Noble and Gerald Shinn. Oxford: Blackwell, 1971.

Harnack, Adolf von. *Geschichte der altchristlichen Litteratur bis Eusebius.* Vol. 1: *Die Überlieferung und der Bestand.* Leipzig: J. C. Hinrichs, 1893.

———. *The Mission and Expansion of Christianity in the First Three Centuries.* Trans. James Moffatt. New York: G. P. Putnam's Sons, 1908.

Heil, Christoph. *Die Ablehnung der Speisegebote durch Paulus: Zur Frage nach der Stellung des Apostels zum Gesetz.* Weinheim: Beltz Athenäum, 1994.

Hengel, Martin. "Zwischen Jesus und Paulus: Die 'Hellenisten,' die 'Sieben' und Stephanus (Apg 6:1-15; 7:54-8:3), *ZThK* 72 (1975) 151–206.

———. *Zur urchristlichen Geschichtsschreibung.* Stuttgart: Calwer Verlag, 1984.

———. *Acts and the History of Earliest Christianity.* Trans. John Bowden. Philadelphia: Fortress, 1980.

———. "Jakobus der Herrenbruder—der erste Papst?" in Erich Grässer and Otto Merk, eds., *Glaube und Eschatologie.* Tübingen: J.C.B. Mohr [Paul Siebeck], 1985, 71–104.

———. "Der vorchristliche Paulus," in idem and Ulrich Heckel, eds., *Paulus und das antike Judentum.* Tübingen: J.C.B. Mohr [Paul Siebeck], 1991, 177–291.

———. "Die Stellung des Apostels Paulus zum Gesetz in den unbekannten Jahren zwischen Damaskus und Antiochien," in James D. G. Dunn, ed., *Paul and the Mosaic Law.* Tübingen: J.C.B. Mohr [Paul Siebeck], 1996, 25–51.

———, and Anna Maria Schwemer. *Paul Between Damascus and Antioch: The Unknown Years.* London: S.C.M. Press, 1997.

Hölbl, Günther. *A History of the Ptolemaic Empire.* Trans. Tina Saavedra. London: Routledge, 2001.

Holtz, Traugott. "Der antiochenische Zwischenfall (Galater 2:11-14)," *NTS* 32 (1986) 344–61.

Horn, Friedrich Wilhelm. "Der Verzicht auf die Beschneidung im frühen Christentum," *NTS* 42 (1996) 479–505.

Jeremias, Joachim. *Jerusalem in the Time of Jesus: An Investigation into Economic and Social Conditions during the New Testament Period.* Trans. F. H. and C. H. Cave. Philadelphia: Fortress, 1969.

Klauck, Hans-Josef. *Herrenmahl und hellenistischer Kult: Eine religionsgeschichtliche Untersuchung zum ersten Korintherbrief.* Münster: Aschendorff, 1982.

———. *Magic and Paganism in Early Christianity: The World of the Acts of the Apostles.* Trans. Brian McNeil. Edinburgh: T&T Clark, 2000.

Kollmann, Bernd. *Jesus und die Christen als Wundertäter: Studien zu Magie, Medizin und Schamanismus in Antike und Christentum.* Göttingen: Vandenhoeck & Ruprecht, 1996.

Kümmel, Werner Georg. *Introduction to the New Testament.* Trans. Howard Clark Kee. Nashville: Abingdon, 1975.

Lipsius, Richard Adelbert. *Die apokryphen Apostelgeschichten und Apostellegenden: Ein Beitrag zur altchristlichen Literaturgeschichte.* Vol. II, part 2. Braunschweig: C. A. Schwetschke und Sohn, 1884.

Lüdemann, Gerd. *Paul, Apostle to the Gentiles: Studies in Chronology.* Trans. F. Stanley Jones. Philadelphia: Fortress, 1984.

———. *Early Christianity According to the Traditions in Acts: A Commentary.* Trans. John Bowden. Minneapolis: Fortress, 1989.

———. *The Resurrection of Jesus: History, Experience, Theology.* Trans. John Bowden. London: S.C.M. Press, 1994.

Mitford, Terence Bruce. "Roman Cyprus," *ANRW* II 7,2 (1980), 1285–1384.

———. "The Cults of Roman Cyprus," *ANRW* II 18.3 (1990), 2176–2211.

Norden, Eduard. *Agnostos Theos: Untersuchungen zur Formengeschichte religiöser Rede.* Darmstadt: Wissenschaftliche Buchgesellschaft, 1956.

Oberhummer, Eugen. *Die Insel Cypern: Eine Landeskunde auf historischer Grundlage I: Quellenkunde und Naturbeschreibung.* Munich: T. Ackermann, 1903.

Ollrog, Wolf-Henning. *Paulus und seine Mitarbeiter: Untersuchungen zu Theorie und Praxis der paulinischen Mission.* Neukirchen-Vluyn: Neukirchener Verlag, 1979.

Pesch, Rudolf. *Die Apostelgeschichte I–II.* Neukirchen-Vluyn: Neukirchener Verlag, 1986.

Radl, Walter. "Das 'Apostelkonzil' und seine Nachgeschichte, dargestellt am Weg des Barnabas," *ThQ* 162 (1982) 45–61.

Räisänen, Heikki. "Die 'Hellenisten' in der Urgemeinde," *ANRW* II 26,2 (1995) 1468–1514.

Rau, Eckhard. *Von Jesus zu Paulus: Entwicklung und Rezeption der antiochenischen Theologie im Urchristentum.* Stuttgart: Kohlhammer, 1994.

Reinbold, Wolfgang. "Die 'Hellenisten': Kritische Anmerkungen zu einem Fachbegriff der neutestamentlichen Wissenschaft," *BZ* 42 (1998) 96–102.

Riesner, Rainer. *Paul's Early Period: Chronology, Mission Strategy, Theology.* Trans. Doug Scott. Grand Rapids: Eerdmans, 1998.

Robinson, John A. T. *Redating the New Testament.* London: S.C.M. Press, 1976.

Roloff, Jürgen. *Die Apostelgeschichte.* Göttingen: Vandenhoeck & Ruprecht, 1981.

Schenke, Ludger. *Die Urgemeinde: Geschichtliche und theologische Entwicklung.* Stuttgart: Kohlhammer, 1990.

Schirrmacher, Christine. *Mit den Waffen des Gegners: Christlich-muslimische Kontroversen im 19. und 20. Jahrhundert dargestellt am Beispiel der Auseinandersetzung um Karl Gottlieb Pfanders "Mîzân al-haqq" and Rahmatullâh ibn Halîl al Utmânî al-Kairânawîs "Izhâr al-haqq" und der Diskussion über das Barnabas-evangelium.* Berlin: K. Schwartz, 1992.

Schmithals, Walter. *The Office of Apostle in the Early Church*. Trans. John E. Steely. Nashville: Abingdon, 1969.

———. *Die Apostelgeschichte des Lukas*. Zürich: Theologischer Verlag, 1982.

———. *The Theology of the First Christians*. Trans. O. C. Dean, Jr. Louisville: Westminster John Knox, 1997.

Schneider, Gerhard. *Die Apostelgeschichte I–II*. Freiburg: Herder, 1980/1982.

Schnelle, Udo. *Wandlungen im paulinischen Denken*. Stuttgart: Katholisches Bibelwerk, 1989.

———. *Einleitung in das Neue Testament*. Göttingen: Vandenhoeck & Ruprecht, 1996.

———. *The History and Theology of the New Testament Writings*. Trans. M. Eugene Boring. London: S.C.M. Press, 1998.

Schreiber, Stefan. *Paulus als Wundertäter: Redaktionsgeschichtliche Untersuchungen zur Apostelgeschichte und den authentischen Paulusbriefen*. Berlin and New York: Walter de Gruyter, 1996.

Schürer, Emil. *The History of the Jewish People in the Age of Jesus Christ*. 3 vols. New English version revised and edited by Geza Vermes and Fergus Millar. Edinburgh: T&T Clark, 1973–1987.

Schüssler Fiorenza, Elisabeth. *In Memory of Her: A Feminist Theological Reconstruction of Christian Origins*. New York: Crossroad, 1983.

Sox, David. *The Gospel of Barnabas*. London: Allen & Unwin, 1984.

Taylor, Nicholas. *Paul, Antioch and Jerusalem: A Study in Relationships and Authority in Earliest Christianity*. Sheffield: Sheffield Academic Press, 1992.

Taylor, Justin. "St. Paul and the Roman Empire: Acts of the Apostles 13–14," *ANRW* II 26,2 (1995) 1189–1231.

Theissen, Gerd. "Hellenisten und Hebräer (Apg 6:1-6): Gab es eine Spaltung der Urgemeinde?" in Hermann Lichtenberger, ed., *Geschichte—Tradition—Reflexion*. Vol. 3: *Frühes Christentum*. Tübingen: J.C.B. Mohr [Paul Siebeck], 1996, 323–43.

Vielhauer, Philipp. *Geschichte der urchristlichen Literatur: Einleitung in das Neue Testament, die Apokryphen und die Apostolischen Väter*. Berlin and New York: Walter de Gruyter, 1975.

Wander, Bernd. *Trennungsprozesse zwischen Frühem Christentum und Judentum im 1. Jahrhundert n.Chr.: Datierbare Abfolgen zwischen der Hinrichtung Jesu und der Zerstörung des Jerusalemer Tempels*. Tübingen: Francke, 1994.

Wehnert, Jürgen. *Die Reinheit des 'christlichen Gottesvolkes' aus Juden und Heiden: Studien zum historischen und theologischen Hintergrund des sogenannten Aposteldekrets*. Göttingen: Vandenhoeck & Ruprecht, 1997.

Wehr, Lothar. *Petrus und Paulus—Kontrahenten und Partner: Die beiden Apostel im Spiegel des Neuen Testaments, der Apostolischen Väter und früher Zeugnisse ihrer Verehrung*. Münster: Aschendorff, 1996.

Weiser, Alfons. *Die Apostelgeschichte*. 2 vols. Gütersloh and Würzburg: Gütersloher Verlagshaus Gerd Mohn, 1981, 1985.

Zimmermann, Alfred F. *Die urchristlichen Lehrer: Studien zum Tradentenkreis der διδάσκαλοι im frühem Urchristentum*. Tübingen: J.C.B. Mohr [Paul Siebeck], 1988.